MAKING IT
COUNT

*Putting Meaning Back in
Business and Relationships*

BRYAN HURLBUT

Synergy Books

Making It Count: Putting Meaning Back in Business and Relationships
Published by Synergy Books
P.O. Box 80107
Austin, Texas 78758

For more information about our books, please write to us, call 512.478.2028, or visit our website at www.synergybooks.net.

Publisher's Cataloging-in-Publication
(Provided by Quality Books, Inc.)

Hurlbut, Bryan.
    Making it count : putting meaning back in business and relationships / Bryan Hurlbut.
    p. cm.
    LCCN 2007939455
    ISBN-13: 978-1-934454-13-8
    ISBN-10: 1-934454-13-3

    1. Success--Psychological aspects. 2. Success in business. 3. Interpersonal relations.   I. Title.

BF637.S8H87 2008   158.2
                        QBI07-600291

Cover concept design by Priyanka Kodikal.

10 9 8 7 6 5 4 3 2 1

I dedicate this book to my beautiful wife, Mary. God certainly smiled on me the day you entered my life. There will never be an adequate way to return the love you give me or to express my heart of gratitude for your support, your kindness and your trust. Thank you for allowing me to chase after my dreams. You are my beloved.

I dedicate this book to Landon and to Abigayle. I love you both more than you can know. I'm proud of you: who you are becoming and who you have become. It is an honor to be your father.

Finally, I am grateful to my Savior without whom I would not be experiencing the life I now have. Jesus, I dedicate this work to You and into Your care. May You be pleased with it and find a place to use it to further Your purpose on this earth. It is my desire to honor You with its publication.

TABLE OF CONTENTS

ONE

EVERYONE LOVES TO TEACH

It seems that no matter where I go and no matter what crowd I fall into, I am always the one who has to walk up and introduce myself to others. Without using all of my fingers and toes, I can easily count the number of times that a complete stranger has walked up to me and started a conversation. Beginning a new job, supporting a new client, or going to a convention all yield the same result. It does not matter where I am; I am passed by the same way: as though I were a chair or part of the foliage in the room. But now that I have embraced the concept that "Everyone loves to teach," I am able to ignite conversation in others and to differentiate myself from the crowd. I do this without fear, with great anticipation, and I enjoy great rewards for doing so.

Loneliness has no company in this wonderful place, as a young friend of mine recently discovered when he started his new position as a chef at an upscale restaurant. The culinary team he joined was tight-knit. A number of them had worked together for years and carried regular conversations. The rest of them knew better than to talk when they shouldn't. "How do I get them to talk with me? No one even tries," was the question he issued me. Here was my response: "Everyone loves to teach, and everyone loves to talk about himself. Get started on either of these two topics, and you won't be able to stop them." The next day, I got a phone call. Just as predicted, he queried one of his managers about his childhood, and for the next twenty minutes, he was treated to a deeper understanding of that man's life and soul.

That is one type of person: one who is willing to be open and transparent. But, I've found that this strategy works when I deal with people who are closed-off controlmongers as well. When I want to establish a common platform so that a controlmonger and I can communicate together long-term, I invest in our relationship by asking him to teach me something. I don't do this in a condescending way, and even if I'm familiar with the process he is teaching me, I use that knowledge to enhance my ability to ask questions. I don't use my existing knowledge to impress him or to express that I already know what he is teaching. Rather, I let him steer the boat, and I go along for the ride, being sure to ask questions along the way so that he has the chance to reveal something.

If you work in any kind of sales capacity, you should be using this skill all the time. When you approach a prospective customer, you should never ask, "May I help you?" That gives the customer an easy out. All he has to say is, "No. I'm just looking." At this point, you're done. What else can you do? If you try to create more conversation, you run the risk of frustrating your customer. Basically, you get one chance and one chance only. If you frivol it away, you may never see it again.

A better way to approach that first attempt is to say, "You know, we have that item in blue, green, and white. What's your favorite color?" For the customer to reply "No. I'm just looking" is out of line and is uncomfortable for him. Because it is uncomfortable, he feels that he must first answer your question. You've just crossed the first stage of communicating with your customer. You've honored him by being concerned about his tastes, and you've asked him to teach you something about himself that you don't yet know.

The phrase, "Everyone loves to teach" started carrying weight with me as a teenager. When I was about fourteen years old, my high school sponsored a fundraiser. The person who sold the most boxes of little candy-dipped chocolate morsels would win a beautiful, brand-new cassette-tape player. But this was no ordinary tape player. After all, it was the eighties. This tape player had a new gizmo called a CD player built into it. Who could have imagined that for a little legwork and a small time investment, a fledgling freshman such as I could win his very own, brand-spanking-new CD player? I had no way of making the cash it took to buy one. So, I was determined to do what it took to win the prize and be the first kid on my block to show it off. I spent hour upon hour going door-to-door, but I barely sold anything. It was horrible. I could feel that majestic, technical wonder slipping rapidly through my fingers. I kept on trying to sell the candy, but my efforts were to no avail. After the first week, I recall having only sold a mere forty boxes of candy.

Then one day, I knocked on the door of a somewhat shabby, broken-down trailer. An older gentleman answered the door—he had to have been at least seventy-one years old, albeit at fourteen, anyone over the age of fifty looked seventy-one to me. Once the door was opened and I had his attention, I started in on my philanthropic spiel that had yielded me such breathtaking results thus far. Finally, when I asked him, "Would you like to buy a box?" he retorted with a very quick and somewhat snide no.

Because I feared my dad would appear out of thin air if I mistreated an older citizen, I bit my tongue and offered a "Thank you anyway," as I started off his front porch. Then, from behind me, he asked, "Don't you want to know why?" Now, having gone to the nursing home many times with my mom to visit my great-uncle, I knew that any time a senior citizen wanted to talk, you were supposed to pretend like you cared and listen politely. In my head I was thinking, "Man! Not now! It's already late. It's getting dark, and I have to be home pretty soon." But, because of my upbringing, I relented and decided to humor the old chap. That was one of the best decisions I have ever made. I was listening out of some kind of self-righteous requirement to honor my family name, but the man at the door was ready to teach.

What I didn't know was that this wonderful older gentleman had been a vacuum-cleaner salesman for thirty years. He had made his living selling something that by that point in our country's history could have been purchased at any department store in the nation. He taught me how to present my goods, how to make them appealing to my potential client, and how to ask for the final sale. He spent more than twenty minutes with me that night while I stood just inside his door. He really worked with me—even making me rehearse what I should say and how I should ask for the sale, so that he could listen and refine my pitch. When I was done, I shook his hand and walked away, genuinely thanking him for his time. Something special had just happened, and as I crossed the threshold back into the brisk night air, a new confidence arose in my bones. His words had changed me.

Over the next two hours, even though I knew I would get into trouble for getting home so late, I went from door to door selling the individual boxes of candy. I told the person answering the door who I was, what the money would be used for, and how I appreciated his or her support. I then gave a couple of suggestions on how the candy could be used, such as in cookies and in freshly popped and buttered popcorn. Finally, I would ask for the sale: "Would you like to buy three or four boxes? They're only fifty cents apiece." To the honor of that older gentleman who took the time to share his life with me, I sold a total of 943 boxes of candy over the next two weeks, and I did so with little to no effort whatsoever. How did I accomplish these phenomenal sales? The older man loved to teach, and I made the decision to listen.

The phrase "Everyone loves to teach" is two-sided and yields a rich reward. Here are some suggestions on how to employ it:

1. Always be real. People can see through any pious attempt to lord over them by using canned psychological mantras. If you can't honestly ask a person about himself, if you can't ask him to teach you something, if you just don't care, then bypass this entire topic and go on. If, on the other hand, you believe in your heart that it's possible to learn something from anyone and if you are willing to let your guard down and listen, this

strategy will open the door to people's souls like nothing else can.

2. Always be ready. While you may ask someone to teach you when it is convenient for you, sometimes the opportunity presents itself when you least expect it. Even in those times, be willing to stop and listen. You never know how it may change your life.

3. Always listen attentively. When people begin to let down their guards and to expose themselves emotionally or historically, that person should be treated kindly and with respect. Maintain eye contact with the person and attentively listen to what he or she is saying. Not doing this is like slapping someone in the face with a glove and humiliating him—even if no one else is around to witness it. Once you ask him to teach you and the person agrees to continue his conversation, he is saying, "I trust you with myself." Failing to listen will deliver a staunch blow to his person. If you ask and don't listen, you shouldn't expect to regain that person's trust in the future.

4. Always look beyond what is being said. Sometimes people say things like, "It was very difficult" or "Yeah. Well, anyway…" Use these types of generalizations to ask for clarification. Don't be afraid to talk. Sometimes people say these things because they want to see if you care enough to dig deeper. If people really begin to feel uncomfortable, they'll let you know. If you're very sensitive about going any further, you can always preface your request with, "If this is too sensitive for you, please don't feel like you have to answer, but…" Sometimes people pull back because the hurt goes deep or because they don't know if they can trust you. Blazing on past these points may open up a wonderful relationship if you are ready for it. I have found that if you are genuine, sincere, and willing to open your life to them, they will give you the same trust, and you may establish a friend for life.

5. Never teach back. If people want you to teach them, they will

ask you. Please, don't ever listen to someone and then use his or her openness as an opportunity to try and turn the tables and teach something in return. An example of this could be with your manager. If you want her to recognize how knowledgeable you are, don't ask, "Miss Williams, would you please show me your method for tracking the movement of widgets?" and then when she's done, retort with, "Well, I was thinking, if we change this and that we could make it more profitable." Bad form. Act honestly, and act because you really want to learn about the person, not for selfish gain.

TWO

IT'S NEVER YOU AND ME

As a young businessman just out of college and starting a new career, I was granted a boss whose investment in me was exceptional. I caused that poor man incessant grief during the time he tried to teach me the lesson found behind the title of this chapter. I wouldn't be surprised if he was taking powerful antidepressant drugs during my early employment with him, but I am elated that he persevered and did not write me off as unsalvageable.

Starting my career as a junior associate at a consulting firm was a real treat. My employer became familiar with me through the work I had done during my college years. When I graduated, he approached me and asked if I would come and join his team. After some pondering, I decided to take the chance, and the opportunity, to do just that.

He dealt continually with my extreme pride and immaturity, and I'm amazed that he allowed me to keep my job for nine years. Over and over, I was determined to prove that I was right. I didn't like to be wrong. I was pretty good at arguing my point and twisting things around so that no matter which way I was falling, I'd still land on my feet by the time I hit the ground. As you can imagine, that made for a number of pretty sad arguments throughout the course of my first professional years. But, through it all, my boss was willing to be patient with me until I was delivered from the demons of pride and self-righteousness. He would give me a metaphorical spanking when I would fall back into my old ways. Every time, his goal for me was the same: he wanted to produce something better in me.

For the rest of this chapter (and book, for that matter) to make sense, it's important to note how the roots of my poor behavior began. I was what most people would consider an underachiever in my younger years. I hated high school because it was boring. I had few friends that I hung around, and I didn't like to be in crowds. To break myself out of this, I started to get involved in drama and other public-speaking events. My hope was that I could break out of my shell and become confident in my ability to communicate. I hoped that some doors of opportunity would open for me. My grades certainly didn't do me any good. At my high school graduation, I walked across the stage with a 2.3 GPA. In a matter of weeks, I loaded up what I could fit into my little Honda Prelude and traveled across the country, anxious to leave the last six years of my life behind me. During that time, I was led through a number of experiences that flushed out some of my pride—living in poverty and eating peanut butter and rice for two months was one of them.

When I came to my senses and realized that I couldn't live on $900 a month, I decided to move home and go to college, flying in the face of all of those who had teased, cajoled, and ridiculed me. There, I flourished. I was determined to make something of myself and to find a way to refine and hone my logic and argumentative skills. I was in heaven. I was finally able to choose what I wanted to do, take the classes I wanted to take, and study when I wanted to study. It was here I discovered that the harder I worked, the more I was rewarded. By nature I am extremely competitive, and so all through college I was determined to earn higher grades than everyone else—yet one more attempt to prove my worth. In some of my classes, I had done so much work that I could have failed the final and still made an A in the class. By the time I was done, I had graduated summa cum laude with a 4.0 GPA and was on my way into the working world, determined to change it and to prove my worth along the way.

My boss sensed this drive in me, and as a result, he gained a very productive and profitable associate. However, he still had to deal with my inability to admit I was wrong when pressed with a challenging issue. When cornered, I always retorted with words like "I" and "you" in a defensive manner and tone, feeling that "I" had to stand my ground and prove that "you" were the cause of the problem. This was something that had to be worked out of me or, more appropriately, ground out of me.

You've probably seen the heavy equipment that is used when a new roadway is being constructed. One of those pieces of heavy equipment is for compaction of the ground, and it looks much like a giant barrel with teeth all over it. Back and forth, back and forth, they drive that piece of equipment over the ground to create a stable underpinning for the new thoroughfare that will be laid upon it. In the same way, over and over again, my boss would tell me, "Never say 'you did this and I did that'; never say 'you said' or 'I told you'. Always use 'us' and 'we' instead of 'you' and 'me.'"

When walking into tense situations, I was always ready for a fight. In my understanding, our type of business wasn't rocket science; we did the work and the client paid the bill. What type of pompous, egomaniac client should peradventure assume he had any right not to pay? In my eyes, the system was simple. There were no strings attached, no hitches, no problems. It was a simple equation of A=B. But, the eyes of the clients were not nearly as myopic. On their side, they looked well beyond the bill. They had powerfully destructive weapons known as assumptions and expectations, and whether or not we met them was a matter of interpretation from their point of view, not from ours.

> They had powerfully destructive weapons known as assumptions.

Needless to say, I created a lot of messes early in my career, and it's amazing that we didn't lose the clients we had. My boss was amazing at lowering himself, and the bill, to keep those clients happy. But even during the times when he had to humiliate himself and sometimes take a lower rate, he didn't give up on me. After a year of constant drilling, I finally started to use the pronouns "us" and "we," and every time I forgot to use them, my 5'3" manager was standing beside me, making certain that I knew he had heard me.

Over time, I learned that changing these few simple words would keep the clients at ease and assure them that we were in the situation together and that we were more interested in them than their bank accounts. We would show them by our language that we were a team and were willing to share in the profit, as well as the loss, of the task. By the end of my third year, I had become quite skilled at using "us" and "we" instead of "you" and "me." It had even gotten to the point that he trusted me to carry conversations on behalf of the association without his needing to be there. I certainly was amazed at the difference two word-switches could make. Never would I have imagined that such a small modification could yield so great a difference. Grudgingly, and still slightly against character, I was forced to yield and to admit that he was right. The fact that after nine years of business we were still servicing the same basic set of clients proved that his instructions were true.

If you find yourself constantly trying to defend your pride, competitiveness and inability to admit you are wrong by hiding behind the words "you" and "me" instead of the words "us" and "we," then here are some useful strategies:

1. Identify the source. Do you feel that you have to defend yourself constantly because you can't be wrong? Do you feel that it's weak to be wrong? Is it competition? Is it fear? Is it that you don't want people to know you are unable to perform your duties? Is it that you don't want others to know the real you? What is it that feeds your need to be right and to show it by using phrases like, "If you'd have done this better, it wouldn't have happened!" Or, "I told you it should be like this. Next time maybe you'll listen." Whatever the base cause of these outcroppings, find it and grind

it into powder. Using these types of jabs shows a lack of caring, a lack of concern and a willful selfishness.

2. Share the hurt. Try to empathize with those in the problem situation; communicate that you are in the battle with them— that you are for them, not against them—even if the problem was their own doing. Use phrases like, "We went into this with assumptions, and we all missed a few that were necessary. Let's identify them and keep going." Or, "We discussed this together and the decision was made to go ahead anyway. Well, here we are, and it didn't work. Shall we revisit the issues once more?"

3. Kill the lion of competition. You will never win a battle by fighting if the victory is found only in death. Lay down your armor and be willing to take the shots. Then, respond with a sentence like, "I can see that you feel strongly about this. We will work together to resolve it. What can we do to make this right?" Often, people strike out because they deal with the same struggles that you do. The fact that someone uses words like "you" and "me" instead of "us" and "we" should tell you that they haven't crossed the bridge to team-centric freedom; they are still trying to prove themselves. But, as long as you are unwilling to compete and unwilling to see whose wit is the strongest—to see who has the deepest longevity—you have nothing to lose. Let them blow, then draw the attention back to the topic at hand and keep going.

4. Embrace discomfort. You may as well get used to the idea that situations will be uncomfortable. If you don't like uncomfortable situations, then you'll never advance in your business, career or even in life. Despite your best intentions, that discomfort will come, and you will have to turn the tide, help people deal with it and draw them together as a team once again. If you learn to see the signs of discomfort and use the energy of that discomfort in a positive way, it will make the process much easier. When in doubt, listen nine times more than you speak and then, through the discomfort, bring the passions and frustrations of the people back into focus.

5. Humble yourself. One sure way to greatly decrease, shorten or eliminate loud, boisterous arguments is to humble yourself before your antagonist. Apologize for any misunderstandings; ask their forgiveness for any wrongs; assure them that your priority is to bring peace to the situation; offer yourself to them and ask them what you need to do in order to straighten out the situation and make it right in their eyes. Whatever you do, make certain that you maintain a quiet demeanor and a willingness to listen. Never, ever interrupt.

6. Be willing to pay. It may be that you have to give a portion of your profits back; perhaps you have to work extra hours or donate your time in some other fashion. Whatever the system of trade, be willing to pay something if necessary. While it's true that you may lose a little time or profit, if doing so will calm people's anxieties, you will probably maintain that relationship for much longer. Don't ever consider it a loss.

THREE

NO TICKIE, NO SHIRTIE

There is someone in everyone's life who invests in them like no one else has ever done. In my life, I've enjoyed a few people like this. One of these people in my life is Mr. Schatz. I had the honor of working with him for thirteen years. His employer contracted with me to manage their Information Technology department. Since Mr. Schatz was the CFO, and since the CFO often gets laden with the IT concerns of the organization, he was stuck working with me.

Over the years, he and I became close friends, and during this time, I gleaned bits of wisdom from him that I have continued to rely upon to this day. These bits of wisdom manifested themselves in his speech as quips and slogans that I have named "Schatzisms." "No Tickie, No Shirtie" is one of my favorite Schatzisms.

For those who are familiar with the oriental laundry experience, "No Tickie, No Shirtie" pulls on a familiar heartstring; it exhumes a certain type of emotion that is otherwise veiled behind the cobwebs of forgetfulness and hidden in the shadows of repression. Certainly you have experienced it or something close to it.

It's 7:53 a.m., you have thirty-seven minutes to pick up your laundry from the cleaners and then to clear the forty-five minute drive through morning traffic in only thirty minutes. You park in the "loading and unloading" zone, just behind the sign that says "5-minute parking," and you rush through the front door. A pleasant, older gentleman comes to the counter of this business, which you have frequented faithfully for the past seventeen years, and asks for your ticket. Your hands fumble around in your pockets and, like lightning in the midnight sky, you realize that you've left your claim ticket on the nightstand beside your bed. "This shouldn't be a big deal," you whisper to yourself as you stand there facing the man you have supported for the past seventeen years. Through your cleaning bills alone, you've paid for at least two of his children to go through college and you've put food on his table as well. You finally decide to put your trust in the fact that you have a solid relationship with each other and you ask the unthinkable. But, no matter how hard you try, and despite your fierce tone of voice, he is unwavering in his position. As you stand there, eye-to-eye and toe-to-toe, nothing you say or do grants you the right to pry your precious items of clothing from his clenched and shaking fists.

So how does it end? You say a few choice words about how you're going to take your business elsewhere, you turn your back on the man you've supported for almost two decades and you galumph out to your car. You yank open the door and then plummet your body into the driver's seat, only to have your view obstructed by a yellow envelope tucked under your driver-side windshield wiper.

What do you learn from this experience? Is it never to use that cursed cleaner again? No. Once you deposit the yellow envelope onto the passenger-side seat and slam your car into drive, your body temperature starts to drop the twenty degrees back to 98.6 and you realize the value of "No Tickie, No Shirtie."

Whether it is your job's duties or dealing with a botched household utility bill, you learn how important documentation is in your life. You learn that knowing where to find the documentation later can reduce your stress and may be of life-altering importance. You learn that there are laws of accountability that supersede business relationships. Here are some tips on how to make certain those repressed feelings of anger and deep frustration stay repressed:

1. Log a response. In day-to-day business situations, when you are done with a meeting, make a habit of sitting in front of your computer and generating a letter or e-mail that starts something like this: "Hey. Thanks for meeting with me. The following is what I took away from our meeting. If you read through this and see that I've misunderstood anything that you said, or if you feel that I need more clarity on any of the following, please give me a call so that we can discuss it further." Then, transfer your notes to the document. This accomplishes a few things:

First, it gives everyone who was in the meeting the opportunity to see what you think they said. Second, it honors them by showing that you cared enough about them and about their information to take notes. Third, it keeps the playing field level. If anyone in the meeting comes back at a later date and says, "You should have known that," you can go back to this document and check to see if you missed something. If you still believe you're right, then you can refer to the document that you sent them and politely ask why they didn't correct your understanding at the time. More than likely, something changed after the meeting and you weren't informed of this change.

While truth never changes, people's perceptions and decisions often do as they glean more information over time. By being polite and apologetic, you give them the ability to preserve their own dignity and to bring you up to speed on information you may not be aware of. Never use this opportunity as a springboard to say, "I'm right and you're wrong." Always give the other person room to be wrong and the opportunity to make the situation right without feeling condemned.

This also works as a great historical resource so that if you ever have to go back and trace a thought process, you have good documentation on how you got from point A to point Z. And finally, it sets you apart from everyone else. How many people do you know who care enough to go the extra step and make certain that they understand what *you* mean?

2. Take extra care in sensitive situations. If you have to deal with an issue that is very sensitive—you know, the kind that makes you sweat and causes your right eye to twitch—and that issue involves dealing directly with "the enemy," here are a few things to try:

A. If the conversation is over the phone, record your helper's name and ID or phone extension. Write these items down, along with the date and time you began your conversation. Don't talk about anything else until you have recorded these pieces of information. Do it on a blank piece of notebook paper or in an electronic document and allow plenty of room for notes.

Asking for this type of personal contact information at the beginning of a conversation will force the person on the other end to decide if he wants to deal with you because it shows how serious you feel about your problem. It also communicates that you expect accountability from him when your conversation is complete. If he gets scared and decides to hang up on you, you're better off. It is ten times better to have him do this at the beginning of a conversation than to get nowhere and have him do it later on; it's also fruitless to deal with someone who doesn't want to deal with you. You need someone who is not afraid to listen to your frustrations and who will help you walk through them. If it means calling back three times until you find someone who is unafraid, at least you know that you will be able to work as a team.

B. When your conversation is complete, be certain to record the ending time. Keeping track of how much energy you had to spend resolving an issue can be helpful later on if it involves the adjustment of time, billing or both. It is also valuable information if you are questioned by authorities at your job. Being able to prove the amount of time you've spent in problem resolution can save your tail. But be careful. If you are ineffective at dealing with a situation, ask for help. Spending 22 ½ hours on something that should have been resolved in three is a loss to your employer that may not offset the resolution of the problem.

C. Determine that you will record and use the information you obtain during your experience in an unemotional way. Emotions are a destructive force when you are dealing with sensitive issues. Don't record things like, "This guy is a jerk" or "The moron said...." Recording things in this fashion only cements the emotion in your head. Instead, record, "Alan was very unhelpful because he wouldn't listen to my request." Then, if you have to go back and recite your notes to someone higher in the food chain, you won't rekindle any more emotion than you absolutely must.

D. Be certain that you take responsibility and state that you may be the problem. When your helper hears that it's not a battle to prove who is innocent, they will be the more ready to help.

3. Group common documents together. Keep all the documents and notes that you accumulate together with the contract, bill or other source document in question. Having it all handy and together will pay off if you have to revisit the issue later. If necessary, make copies of your source documents so that the originals end up where they're supposed to; that way you won't be holding up the rest of the process if the originals are required.

FOUR

FAULT TOLERANCE

You are driving through East St. Louis at 10:12 p.m. in the middle of the worst rainstorm you have seen in years when all of a sudden there's a complete blackout. There are no street lights, no warning signs, nothing. The only things that are emitting any luminance at all are the head and tail lights of the cars around you. Little by little, traffic slows to an excruciating crawl as people slow down in an attempt to find their exits. As you continue on, you find what you believe to be yours and, in a leap of faith, turn your signal on to warn all other gropers that you are getting ready to make your way out of the blind maze.

As you drive down the street, you see nothing familiar. The street lights that once explained where you were by casting their dull glow on the houses, stores and street signs beneath them are nowhere to be seen. Slowly, you drive through a suburban shopping area just outside your neighborhood—you know, the little strip mall with the small grocer and the liquor store. Everything seems eerie to you because it's as though you've stepped out of your familiar world into a silent world of death—there is no sign of life, no activity of any kind. Everyone has their doors and windows closed; no one is

> **It's as though you've stepped out of your familiar world into a silent world of death.**

walking on the streets; the traffic is almost non-existent; it is just you and a motorcycle across the way. But wait, with your peripheral vision you see a faint glow in the grocery store to your right. Hoping that the electricity will come on soon, you veer into the parking lot and wait for a few minutes to see if your hope manifests. This gives you the chance to be first in line when the lights come back on so that you can get your much-needed bread, eggs and milk before hitting the front door of your house and calling it an exhausting day.

As you pull in front of the little shack, you discover that it's not the staff, but looters who have broken through the glass to take what they want. You slam your transmission into reverse, and, using only the dimness of your red tail lights, are able to drive all the way to the street without hitting anything. Shaken, you throw it into drive and head home. You mumble to yourself, "How can people turn into such fiends? They wouldn't act this way if the lights were on!"

As you finally make it home, you pull into your parking stall and find everyone in your complex hiding in complete fear, afraid to open their doors. The only sign of life is the faint glow of candles and flashlights, which cast dancing shadows on the blinds that cover the windows. Just as you step out of your car, the street lights around you perk up and in seconds are at full beam. You watch as doors and windows begin to open up to the fresh breeze that has been blowing all night long—a breeze that you had been enjoying all the way home. You watch traffic begin to flow smoothly along the street in front of your apartment. Only a few minutes later, you see kids riding their skateboards and people walking hand-in-hand, laughing and enjoying each other's company as though nothing had happened.

This is a perfect example of what happens when a system of any kind fails. Whether it is electrical, mental, physical or informational, the same basic repercussions will happen to any entity when its life-giving flow is cut off. Traffic begins to slow and sometimes stop completely. Direction is lost. Fear sets in. People shut down and lock themselves in their safety zones. The evil tendencies inside of some are loosed due to fear and anticipation of the worst. The question is, how can you stop that life-giving flow from being cut off in the first place? And if you can't stop it from being cut off, how do you limit the repercussions?

An entire series of books could be written on this topic, and indeed several have been. The point here is not to cover every minute bit of information necessary to stop meltdown from happening in your life or work, but to give you a few simple rules that will cover the majority of situations you will come across in your short existence here on Earth. For the sake of universality, we will use the word "entity" to describe you as an organization or as an individual. Every entity has form, personality and life flow. As an example, life flow for an organization is its information. For the human body, life flow is its blood. So, interpret the word "entity" in whatever context you may be reading from.

Each entity can change only so much at any single point in its life. Each entity handles change differently based on its composition, its resilience and its flexibility. When any entity is changed, either repetitively or constantly, there is no way for healing time to occur. If you take any human and perform a serious operation on his body every couple of weeks and continue to do so for a complete year, the chances are extremely good that by the end of a year, that person will have expired. Businesses are no different. If you continue to operate and to change without allowing an ample amount of healing time, you may not have a business when you are done.

Have you ever reached a point in your life where you said, "This is too much. I can't take it anymore. If another thing happens to me, I'm done. I'll quit"? This is the point of low–fault tolerance. You have pushed your system, your health and your stress level to the maximum, and without some kind of healing time, you may not be able to continue. There are entire wards of hospitals dedicated to people who have not heeded the signs of system failure and have pushed themselves past their fault-tolerant point. If you're a business, take this situation and multiply it by the seventy-eight other people working in the same department. Since each person is constructed differently in his or her ability to handle load and stress, not everyone is feeling the same level at the same time. Indeed, there are those who will never feel any stress at all because they simply don't care. But, among the caring lot, as soon as you see one person exhibit low-fault-tolerance signs, it's a guarantee that there are others reaching the same point, and if change continues on without rest, more will follow.

A client of mine recently went through a huge transition when employees occupying a handful of higher positions in the organization changed. In the words of the president of that corporation, "When there is a change in the leadership of an organization, by necessity there comes a change in direction." In their case, that change in direction was executed very swiftly and with little visible concern for their employees. During that time of change, people who were close to retirement were terminated. Others who were valuable to the organization were demoted so that friends of those now in power could be brought in to fill those positions. None of these things were illegal. However, the morale of the organization began to plummet over the next few months. As change after change continued to occur, people began to wonder about their jobs. "After all, if so-and-so has worked here for seventeen years and was just released, what chance do I have to keep my job?" Seeds of fear and humiliation were sown as the decision was made to escort employees out of the building upon their dismissal. People who had been employed by this company for years and who had been trusted only moments before were publicly shamed and told to wait outside the building until their personal effects were brought to them. Distrust between employees and toward their managers ensued, and the organization swiftly headed down the road toward an atmosphere where employees were self-consumed and looked out only for themselves.

This is a perfect example of how change can be executed poorly. So much change happened so quickly that the general body of the organization had no time to recuperate, no time to trust the character and intentions of their new leadership, no time to see how the changes that had already happened would function. Instead, when this type of change takes place, people begin to do their jobs out of fear; they shut down and secure themselves behind secure doors and close their windows so that they can't be hurt. They create subversive allegiances with those who they trust implicitly and who won't betray them. They carry on conversations with no one else because they fear that if they open the door to talk, that person may end up being a looter who will take advantage of them and then create even more fear, betrayal and destruction in their life. Every time this happens, it lowers the threshold of fault tolerance and brings a home, a business, a church or a civic organization closer to failure and possible ruin.

There are times when poor management or situations beyond control can force catastrophes very quickly, and in these cases, there is no way to slow down the rate of change. We just have to be certain that we only change as much as we have to as quickly as we have to in an attempt to give the entity a chance to heal and rest. As a cancer patient, if you find that you are diagnosed with stage-three cancer, your doctor cannot put you on a constant stream of chemotherapy. If she gave you a treatment beyond the proper and tolerable length, your body would shut down and you would die from poisoning. Receive too little, and you would walk away with little improvement. But, administered in the proper dosages at the proper times with the proper controls and the proper amount of rest between treatments, that poison can go through your system and kill the cancerous cells, and you can live a much healthier and longer life.

Here, then, are some strategies to handle change and to enhance your fault tolerance so that system failure will not happen to you:

1. Know your entity. You have to know your entity before you can begin to change. Don't ever assume that you know; be certain that you know. Do whatever research and enlist whatever people are necessary to educate yourself first. If you are a business, invite line staff, and not just managers, to help in the process. Look at your organization from every possible vantage point

before jumping in and making system-wide changes. You may be amazed at how differently your business operates in comparison to how you view it. Don't let your pride determine how your business operates. As an individual, don't be afraid to ask advice from someone who is removed from your situation; even if you have to pay a little money for his input. If it's someone who you trust or who is excellent in his or her field of expertise, it may save you considerable resources later on.

2. Change gradually. Change in accordance with a plan that is carefully drafted and executed. If you can avoid huge amounts of change all at once, you will be better off. Remember the cancer patient example above. Too much chemotherapy too quickly will lead to death. You have to know your patient, know their limits and prescribe a method of change that is commensurate with their capacity to handle change.

3. Communicate. The company I referenced earlier was scared to let the general body of employees know their plan to change, possibly because they feared that people would jump ship. This is understandable in some cases. However, in as much as it is possible, try to communicate with people, letting them know why things are being done. As people are relieved of duties and sent on their way, perception plays a huge part in the lives of those who are left behind. Help alleviate some of the stress by finding ways to communicate with those who remain and do so without adding spin and lies to the mix. People want honesty; they can tell when they are being soft-soaked. Remember: the truth will always outlive a lie.

4. Have a good bedside manner. Be patient with people as they adjust to new positions and new coworkers. Change is tough enough in itself, and people need extra attention, extra encouragement and extra care during transition times. These are the times when people feel the least valued and the most vulnerable. When someone is relieved of their duties due to restructuring, make a point to encourage those left behind; let them know when you are done restructuring their area and when

things will be stable again. If you are the one responsible for making change, fear and uncertainty may not be an issue for you—after all, it's not your job that is in peril. But, to the rest of the employees of that area, their world may have just been drastically shaken. Treat them like dying patients. If they were terminally ill, how would you speak to them? How would you react if they were frustrated or angry? On a personal note, if you, as an individual, decide not to do business with someone, not to volunteer or not to support your civic group, be kind enough to explain why and don't be upset by the reaction of others. Remember, your decision to change has just caused them to change too, and they will need time to adjust.

5. Check for progress often. If you start throwing continuous changes into whatever you are modifying, make certain that you stop to see if your changes are bearing fruit. By failing to stop and evaluate, you have just decreased your fault tolerance by 50 percent.

If you knew that your vehicle had a 50 percent chance of failing, would you use it for a long road trip? For something to increase fault tolerance, it must attack a problem and be monitored for success. In the case of chemotherapy, if you prescribe the amount of chemical you feel is necessary to kill the cancer but you never watch your patient's vital signs during treatment or the effect it has on the cancer after treatment, how will you know if you are eliminating the problem? In the same way, you have to monitor the changes you institute, and you have to do it tenaciously. Don't settle for someone's word that things are fine. Look at the facts. Invite others to look at the facts with you. Talk to representatives on both sides of the change—to those making the changes and to those being changed. Keep a wide base of information and interpretation streaming in. You never know when someone's comments or observations will trigger your next breakthrough.

6. Set goals. Before you start to make changes, you need to set achievable goals and then use creative communication skills to

let those involved know that you and they are on target. Doing this will bring more stability to the minds of those affected and will let them know that you aren't driving uncontrollably and furiously down the hill of change with no visible end in sight. At some point, it will convey that you have achieved your goals and are poised for what lies ahead.

FIVE

A GIFT BY ANY OTHER NAME

You hear a knock at the door and upon opening it, you see a small child holding a fistful of magazines and an empty order sheet. She pitches her sale to you and asks you to support her school by buying one of her wonderful magazines and giving it as a present to your favorite aunt. By the time the transaction is complete, you pat yourself on the back for supporting your local school and for thinking of your dear Aunt Minnie all in the same five-minute period. As a matter of fact, in a fit of selfless generosity, you even buy two magazine subscriptions for yourself. You draw the door closed in front of you and go on with your life. So proud are you of your selfless deed that you walk around the rest of the evening with a smile on your face and a gleeful heart, joyous because you have selflessly supported a small child in her attempt to adjoin philanthropy and capitalism.

As you go to bed that evening, you bask in the light of your selflessness, happy that you were able to give to one in need. As subsequent days go on, you lose track of your selfless deed and are again caught up in life's day-to-day trials and joys. Then, like stray voltage amassing itself into one giant lightning bolt, you are hit with the realization

onths and you still haven't seen the first
iption. You go online and check your
)ast three months to see if the charge
⌐o your befuddlement, you discover
ir card was charged for $57.95 as
)u bought from the little girl. In a
,our top desk drawer and rummage
Jur way past the paperclips, staples and sticky
L⌐ your phone book and call the grade school you were
⌐ered into sponsoring.

Frustrated, you ask for the principal and then when she gets on the phone, you ask why you were charged for magazines that you never received. When she asks you the name of the child who sold them to you and when it was that you purchased the magazines, you obviously can't remember and are now thrown into a semi-cataclysmic state of rage as you struggle to hold onto your words. So shocked you are that they dare insult you by asking things you can't remember and didn't care enough to record at the time. When all is said and done, you have created nothing but a fool of yourself and an opportunity to offer an apology to another one of society's underpaid public servants.

What happened to the feeling of giving? What happened to the selfless act that you performed at the start of this process? Was it really selfless, or were you expecting something in return? If you were really doing it to help the school, would it matter that you ever got the magazines? This is the heart of the issue. When you give—when you support—what are you expecting to get back? Until you give with no expectation of return, you really haven't given at all.

> **Was it really selfless, or were you expecting something in return?**

I had a friend who was a chronic smoker; she had smoked for years and enjoyed doing it. Because I love this lady like my sister, I decided to take some of the profit I was making in my business and to invest it in her. I told her that if she could go three months without smoking, I would pay her $500 and then, if she made it the rest of the year without smoking, I would give her an additional $500. After she realized that I was being brutally truthful with her, she decided to take me up on my offer. Through eighteen packs of nicotine gum and at least two cords of toothpicks, she quit smoking for the first three months. True to form, I wrote her a check for the amount I had offered and I gave it to her. Then she started the rest of her journey.

Over the next nine months, she didn't smoke another cigarette. During that time, I found great joy and pleasure in thinking about how healthy she would be in ten years; how I was affecting her life. As a dad, my children mean everything to me, and so I found myself thinking of her family and the fact that she would certainly enjoy her life with her children even more by quitting the deleterious habit she had developed. Over and again I would encourage her to keep going; I put up with her horrible mood swings and her frustrating arguments—all of this was part of getting off the nicotine. But, to me, the frustrations were worth it. All I had in view was the expectation of seeing her free from the addiction. And, at the end of the nine months, true to my word, I gave her the rest of the promised cash.

From my point of view, I thought I was being handsomely generous. After all, how many people get paid cold, hard cash to stop a bad habit? I was very proud of myself for sacrificing my profits to make the change palatable enough for her to quit. Still, after a few weeks had gone by and I hadn't received the gratitude that I expected, I was a little upset. On top of this, after a total of fifteen months of smoke-free living, she started smoking again. I was livid. I had invested all that time, energy and money into her life and she repaid me by going back to the habit of smoking. After all I had done, to be repaid with such a slap in the face was inexcusable.

After dealing with this issue by myself and getting nowhere, I went to talk with my friend Mr. Schatz, to whom you were introduced in a previous chapter. His advice to me was what broke the situation and released me from the bitter frustration I was experiencing.

Mr. Schatz challenged me and my motive. After all, if I was giving a gift, I should have had no ongoing expectations. My friend did what she said she would do, and I gave what I said I would give. But, I was still holding that gift over her head and waving it in front of her face. The attention failed to be a selfless act of giving. Instead, I was drawing the attention and the focus back to me, the giver. When I realized that I was, indeed, expecting something more for the money I had given, and when I realized that it was not a gift but a bribe to quit smoking, I was amazed. I had been convinced that I was giving selflessly and yet my actions proved this was not so.

It was at that point that I recalled something Jesus said about giving. In one of His times of sharing with those hungry for what He had to offer, He instructed the people to give, expecting nothing in return. He even went so far as to say we weren't to loan anything to anyone but that, instead, we were to give whatever was requested and not to expect it back. Jesus was certainly no fool. For, as I learned in this situation, if you give without expecting anything in return, you have no room for frustration or dashed expectations; you are left only with the pleasant memory of being selfless and heartfelt.

If you are a manager, an employer, a parent, a pastor, a professional or if you give to people in any way and you expect those people to be grateful for your goodness to them, save yourself the tattered heart and adjust your thoughts before it's too late. Choose to be a good and selfless giver because it's right, because it's honorable and because it's godly. Don't do it out of your own need to be needed. Give without expecting anything in return—no thanks, no recognition and no benefit of any kind. When you get to the point where you can give in this fashion, you have become a truly pure giver.

As you work on your pure giving skills, consider the following:

1. Check your motive. When you give, why do you do it? Is it because you want to be appreciated? Is it because you want to engender faithfulness from others? Do you want to earn friends? Whatever the reason, if it's anything other than simple giving

with the sole intent of the other person receiving joy or benefit from the gift, it's not really giving; it's buying or investing.

2. Force out the doubt. When you are first learning how to give, you may doubt yourself considerably. You may even doubt that it's possible to make yourself give selflessly without expectation of return. Don't let that stop you. The only way to learn to give selflessly is by repetition. You do it, and when you see you've failed, you ask God to help you get past your selfishness and then you try again. Just don't give up.

3. Be real. If you are reading this and you feel that you have no problems giving, challenge yourself at every juncture. Each of us has an area somewhere inside us that hurts when we give. We hurt because of something that has happened to us or some area of pride we choose to protect. If you can't see it now, just wait; it will rear its ugly head soon enough, and when you see your expectations raising around a gift you've given, capture those expectations, wad them up and throw them away. Use the experience as your mirror—face yourself, realize you're flawed and go on to the next step.

4. Never quit. No matter what station you may hold in life, never quit working on your skills as a giver. Whether it's time, attention, money or talent, keep working on your giving skills. Don't ever feel that you've mastered the fine art of giving. There's always more to give and there are always better ways of giving. Set yourself up for a challenge. Take something that is your prized possession or an amount of money that makes you grit your teeth when you think of giving it. Then, find someone that needs it more than you do and give it in absolute anonymity. See how you handle the gift when all is said and done. Are you able to give it without anyone ever knowing you did it? Can you keep from telling even your closest friend that it was done? Whatever the case and whatever the response, you should never quit giving. Never stop trying to refine your talent at being the perfect giver.

SIX

WHAT IS TRUTH?

"What is truth?" This quote was made famous in 33 AD by Pontius Pilate, who was a Roman governor. On the shirttails of his doubt, mankind has asked this same question for the past two thousand years, and there are still those who wonder if something known as truth really exists. The Greeks had the meaning of truth hammered out more than any other culture I am familiar with. According to their language experts, truth is the highest form of reality that exists. Once you get to truth, there is nowhere else to go; you have reached the pinnacle of understanding. If this is the case, how can we settle for less? Why wouldn't we continue to push past the fakes and the placebos until we get to the final resting place—a place called truth?

I'm ashamed of the number of times I have traveled down a road toward truth and settled for something less—something that may have seemed more tasty, something that may have been more convenient, something that may have been more easily fought for. When I ponder my ways and think of the people who I've hurt, the gossip I've spread and the lies I've believed, I realize that it's all because I didn't take the time to press on until I arrived at the truth and to pin my tongue to my bottom teeth until I got there.

Working in any group setting brings out the most pleasant and the most wicked side of us all. In group settings you find the beauty of your selfless humanity when you sacrifice for your coworkers and express your love to them through handshakes, pats on the back, hugs, parties, gifts and prayers. You show your commitment to them by proving yourself in difficult times and by giving of yourself even when you are tired and want to go home. Group settings are also the place where we show our bitter, backbiting, self-centered, ego-driven personalities by spinning carefully constructed webs of mistrust, lies, hate, anger and abusive competition.

At about 3:00 p.m. one day, I found myself working in the office alone. One of the younger workers in our association had been out of town for a few days, traveling somewhere for personal business. For the sake of anonymity, let's call him Jack. In the silence of my office I heard the "ding" of my e-mail program notifying me that I had just received a delivery. I used the infamous alt-tab keystroke to bring it up on the screen so that I could read it. I didn't recognize the sender's name, but the e-mail told me about Jack and about some lewd activities that had happened at a party the previous night. The sender of the e-mail had gotten pretty far with his date and wanted to know how well Jack had scored. He was trying to get a hold of Jack but he wasn't having any luck, so he sent an e-mail to me.

After reading the e-mail, I was frustrated that Jack would have tried such things and was shocked that his friend would send me such an e-mail. I really didn't know what to do with it. Should I just delete it and pretend that I didn't get it? Should I respond to the sender in some way? What should I do? After pondering on it for a while, I decided to forward the e-mail to Jack and let him know that his friend was looking for him. Even though Jack and I had worked together for a few years by then, I still didn't feel that it was my place to offer corrective advice or that I had any real place to talk to him about his personal affairs. Yet, the details of the e-mail were so disturbing that I felt if no one ever challenged him on his behavior, it would end up being destructive to him. So, against what I would now call common sense, I wrote the following, "I know this may not mean anything to you, but...."

That was one of the biggest mistakes I have ever made in my life. Here is what I didn't know until well after I had sent the e-mail to Jack. The e-mail that I had received, even though it mentioned Jack by name, was actually misdirected. It turns out that there are a couple of people in the United States with my name. Evidently, someone with the name of Jack went to a party with another man that had the same name as me and they each had had their time frolicking. When all was said and done, a third person at the party who knew Jack and the other "me" didn't know how to get a hold of this other Jack, but he did remember my name—or at least the name of the other man with my name. He did a quick web search and came across my e-mail address, and thinking that I was the other Jack's friend, sent off an e-mail inquiring about what had happened with Jack the night before. For those of you who enjoy reading Shakespeare, it was a real "comedy of errors," although for me, there were no laughs to be found.

Because of my willingness to stop short of the truth and believe what had been handed to me, I created a handful of harmful repercussions: I hurt my reputation; I hurt my developing friendship with Jack; and, I made my employer angrier than anyone I've ever seen before or since. After a scorching e-mail, a spicy phone call from my boss and after I realized that the whole thing was one behemoth misunderstanding on my part, I immediately called Jack and apologized. I explained that I wrote the e-mail out of concern for him and that if I hadn't cared, I would have done nothing. Obviously, that made no difference to him. What I had done was disgraceful, and I don't blame him for his frustration. The repercussions of that experience had such long-lasting effects that I never recovered from them. To this day, when I see Jack, he is cordial to me, but it's obvious that my lack of discretion was a huge stab in his back and a giant gash against his personality. I would rather have left this very embarrassing fault hidden, but I'm exposing it to you because it holds such great value. There is nothing I can do to regain Jack's respect. Quite possibly, it has been lost forever.

Here's one other example that may ring true for you; indeed, we have all been guilty of this. How often do you receive an e-mail from a friend or coworker that seems sensational but believable? How often do you receive an e-mail that, because of your own convictions or passions, is believable without the slightest doubt? Whether the e-mail states that Congress is trying to pass a bill to establish a tax on every e-mail that is sent to offset the lost revenue of the U.S. Postal Service, or it's an e-mail stating the horrible atrocities of our president in his years as a young man, do you check them out before sending them on? I try to make a thorough search on the web to find out if e-mail like these are true or false. At least 95 percent of all of the sensational e-mail I get turns out to be false. When that happens, I reply to the e-mail and politely ask the originator to send the truth back to the people who they had just misinformed by their previous e-mail. I always include links to the facts so that others can inform themselves. I will generally never use the "reply to all" function found in e-mail clients. Doing so shames the sender of an errant e-mail and exposes his ignorance. Remember that when we fail to reach for the truth and instead accept seemingly truthful thoughts without validating them, it destroys our credibility.

By determining to seek the truth, by not giving up until you have found it and by waiting until it's found before taking any action, you will be able to preserve yourself from situations similar to the ones I've described above. Now, here is what I've learned to do:

1. Know the source. If I had done my homework in regard to Jack, I would have first evaluated the source of the information to determine if it was reputable or not. As it was, I took the information that was given to me at face value, and I never looked behind it to see if there was more that could be found. The fact that the e-mail originator's name was foreign to me should have been a red flag. The fact that I was the second generation to hear about the events by the time the e-mail had gotten to me also should have been a red flag. If you don't have first-generation experience with

a situation, you should be all the more leery of believing it until the originator of the experience has actually communicated to you in person.

2. If you want to believe it, beware. There is an old adage about buying investment property. It goes something like, "If you see a house and you feel like you have to have it, walk away right then and save yourself the loss." Any time something seems true and you choose to believe it because you want to believe it rather than checking it out from top to bottom, take it as a sign of impinging danger to you. You are probably stepping into piranha-infested waters. Don't believe something because you choose to believe it. Believe it because it has been proven and can be proven.

3. Always assume you could be wrong. This step took me quite a while to learn. You can't lose if you always assume that you could be wrong. Had I assumed that I was wrong before sending that e-mail to Jack, my forwarded e-mail might have read something like, "Jack, I got this e-mail and it says it's addressed to you. Is this really yours, or do I need to reply to the sender?" Replying like that would have expressed dignity to Jack. It would have also given him the ability to refute the e-mail and preserve his name without being challenged to do so. Remember, if we are truly concerned, we should discuss any sensitive issues in person, privately, at a later date and certainly not by e-mail.

SEVEN

ALWAYS FORGIVE— NEVER FORGET

When I started my computer hardware sales and support business it was with one main goal in mind: I wanted to have money to give to others. I was making a salary that was typical for my field of work, but I seldom had enough money left over to give to the things that deeply moved my soul. Because I wanted a way to raise money to give away, my business took its first breath in October of 1992.

As time went on, my interests began to increase, and so did my computer business; it took more and more hours out of my day to manage and more and more effort to make a profit. I was bidding computer hardware at a profit margin of just 3 percent to get the sale, and I was having fun doing it. During this time, I was still working as an associate for a consulting firm and fulfilling my obligations there. Life was busy—too busy. One day, I decided it was time to make my money work for me instead the other way around. I began contemplating ways to invest the excess cash that I had made, in hopes of making a greater return. I examined the money market, CDs and stocks. Finally, my mind was made up. I decided to invest in stocks and commodities.

I scheduled an appointment with a financial planner and started my education. What I discovered was that even though it made sense to the financial planner, it was Inuktitut to me. I needed someone to come alongside of me, take my money, invest it and keep me up to date with what was happening. I needed someone who I could trust as much as myself and who would help me meet my financial goals. Unfortunately, as much as I liked the financial planner I was with, I didn't have enough money to make him interested in me.

A couple of months passed, and I was still looking for a good financial leader. I was never happier than when a good friend of mine moved back to town and started his own investment firm. He was licensed as a series seven broker and for the past several years he had worked for a major investment company in another state. His family lived just down the street from me. We often spent time together socializing and running in the same circles. Also, the fact that we had known each other since middle school made it even better. I was ecstatic when he told me he had gotten his broker's license in my state and that he was starting his new business closer to home. My heart raced when we began to talk of financial matters because I had finally found someone who could explain things to me in a fashion that made sense and who I could trust.

He introduced me to the coffee, sugar and cocoa markets. He introduced me to industrial bonds. He introduced me to stock options. Because of the education that he gave me, I learned how to ask questions and ultimately, I even learned that the bond market was responsible for setting interest rates on house loans. Because of that, I was able to refinance my house during a change in the market and cut fifteen years off the note with little change in my house payment. It had become a very fruitful financial relationship.

A local company was trying to raise money for capital, and he was working with them to get it off the ground. He approached me about the investment and after some consideration, I decided to try it. It was a short-term investment, and it paid a pretty good interest rate, but when the note came due, they didn't pay. It was the first time in my professional relationship with him that I had lost money. Still, my gain was well over my loss so I didn't let it bother me too much. I kept investing money, and I kept making money. Since there were only a few times that I lost money, I decided to get smart and make higher risk investments.

In essence, I started to pull money from outside sources that I was paying little or no interest on and to invest that money in the hope of making a higher yield. When the investment came in, I would pay off the low rate money and wait for another investment to come along that seemed to fit my interests.

After about three or four months of this kind of senseless activity, it turned out that more and more of my investments were bombing out. Day by day, it became harder to get in contact with my friend and broker; even going by his office yielded few results. When he was there, we had good conversations and he described what was happening as part of the overall experience of investing and stated that I shouldn't give up. However, little by little, the investments kept failing, and I continued to lose more and more money. When, at last, I embraced some miniscule amount of common sense, I came to the conclusion that something was happening under my radar. I

> **The investments kept failing and I continued to lose more and more money.**

decided to start pulling out of the investments so that I could recapture the money I had invested and not lose any more than necessary. By pulling out then, I would net close to zero. So with about $25,000 in outstanding leveraged debt, I began the descent back to normalcy.

Let me digress to a previous time. Let's go back to the day before I started investing with my friend, and I'll share a deeper, more spiritual side of what was happening.

I was very worried and concerned about investing the money I had worked so hard to earn. Well before I ever dreamed of leveraging my business, even before I invested the first $1,000 into options, I was uneasy. I went out one evening and spent time talking with God about what I was about to do. "Lord, I'm not sure why, but I just feel uneasy about investing with my friend. Why should I feel so uneasy?" I asked. But even after a half-hour of soul-searching, I could not think of any reason why I should be concerned. I chalked up my uneasiness to unfounded fears associated with an unknown experience and went on. As the rest of this experience unfolds, you will see that God was trying to be gracious to me and to warn me of pending danger, but because of my greed, I went right on past the road signs and straight off a cliff.

Have you ever had a strange feeling like something out of your control is going to happen? Almost like there was someone constantly trailing you? A feeling so real that you got in the habit of repetitively looking over your shoulder to see if there was, indeed, anyone there? For two months, I lived with this fear. I recall telling my wife that it was like I had botched some deal with the mafia and that some of their henchmen were trailing me, waiting to find the right moment to dress me in a matching ensemble of cement shoes and coat. There was no peace in my home; I got little uninterrupted rest, and it was grating on me. I soon found out why.

My doorbell rang at about 8:30 a.m. one day. Having received a call the previous day, I knew who it was and I wasn't anxiously awaiting his presence in my home. This was a man who scared me just by his position. Due to the fact that he was now standing outside my door, my palms got sweaty and my heart started to race. It was obvious that my fight or flight instinct had just kicked in.

I went to the door and asked for three pieces of identification. He showed me his personal business card, his driver's license and his badge. All three identified him as an agent of the Securities and Exchange Commission. I invited him into my house and offered him a seat. I had already set up my camcorder in the northwest corner of my dining room and told him that I intended to record our entire conversation. He agreed and had no problem with my concerns at all. He opened his satchel and began pulling out papers and books. It was here that I learned first-hand what the word "sequester" means. I found in these papers and books all of my friend's financial records. They had been impounded from all the banks that the Securities Exchange Commission could identify as being used in the misuse of my money. That was a red letter day for my vocabulary usage, as I gained yet another definition for my continued use: Ponzi Scheme. I was deep in one. The American Heritage Dictionary describes Ponzi Scheme as follows: "An investment swindle in which high profits are promised from fictitious sources and early investors are paid off with funds raised from later ones."

Just a couple of weeks before, this man, who I had trusted so deeply, was sitting at my table as a guest in my home eating a wonderful dinner that my wife had prepared for him and that I had paid for. We invited him as a guest into our home because we loved him and cared for him, and because we wanted to show him our gratitude. And now, only a few weeks later, I find that he is using and abusing me, my friendship and my trust—all of which had been established over the course of an eighteen-year relationship.

As the agent from the SEC concluded his three-hour presentation, I was numb. One of the last things he said to me was, "Bryan, I'm sorry. But statistically, you'll be lucky if you get 20 percent of your money back." That meant that if his statistics were accurate, I would have a debt of $21,000 that I would have to pay back with no additional source of income.

The rest of this story may seem a bit unrealistic to you, but you must know that it's 100 percent true.

I spent some time alone gathering my thoughts and thinking about what had happened. I went down the street to talk to my friend and when he answered the door, he told me that he could not speak with me on order of his attorney. No matter how hard I tried to find out what happened, he wouldn't budge. I left his home and spent more time gathering my thoughts. How in the world could I tell my wife that I had taken $25,000 from sources that I would have to repay, that I used it to invest, that I lost it all and now had to repay it with no hope of any help from my friend? How could I have been so naïve? How could I have had such blind trust?

Later that night I went out for a walk. I went back to the same spot in the street, under the same streetlight, at almost the same time of evening where I had made the decision to break past my uneasiness and go ahead with my investing plans. I prayed to God and repented for not listening to His warning and, instead, traipsing into financial torment. I committed the situation to Him and, according to Jesus' command, chose to forgive my friend for what he had done to me.

I believe in the biblical representation of forgiveness as extended to us by Jesus Himself. You may disagree, but don't let a fear of accepting Jesus' authoritative position stop you from seeing the real truth He brings. True forgiveness is not a feeling; it may not even be deserved. True forgiveness is when we can throw away the circumstances, the hurt and the repercussions and look at the offending party as though it never happened. We make the decision to forgive irrespective of his or her willingness to ask us for it because we want that same type of forgiveness for ourselves. I truly believe that unless we have experienced the deep forgiveness that Jesus offers, it is excruciatingly hard, if not impossible, to squeeze true and full forgiveness out of ourselves. I believe with all my heart that without the deepest experience of forgiveness, we have broad difficulties expressing forgiveness to others. Given that this conviction is a core component of my makeup as a person, I knew what needed to happen next.

I met my wife at the house about 5:00 p.m. and started our conversation with the following request: "Sweetheart, I need you to listen to what I'm going to say, and I don't want you to ask any questions until I'm done. When I'm finished explaining what has happened, I'll say, 'I am done' and then I'll answer whatever questions you have." With a very deep breath, I delved into the whole story of my mistake. After about forty-five minutes of explaining everything from start to finish, I paused for her response. All I received from her as a reply was, "Okay. I trust you." You may be thinking that my wife is a nut. But, as a husband who had just made the biggest mistake of his life thus far, it was the best thing I could have heard. My wife was telling me that even though I made a mistake, she forgave me and trusted me to lead my household and my business.

I then told her the next thing on my list, which was to write a letter to my friend. She looked at me like a raccoon in headlights but, true to her words, she let me lead the way I felt I needed to lead. I sat down at my computer and wrote a letter to my friend expressing that I forgave him for stealing from me and that I was giving him the money with no expectation of return—it was a gift from me to him. I took the letter down and had it notarized to make it legal and then walked to his home and handed it to him. I gave him a hug and walked away a free man. While it is true that I still had to pay back the $25,000 debt, this was a minor hurdle compared to my newfound freedom—freedom I had gained by forgiving him, releasing him and going on with my own life. When I made that decision, I told my wife, "My chances are infinitely better to trust God for a return of that money than to trust that I'll be repaid by a thief." My expectations of God's intervention were not thwarted.

After sucking in my pride, I walked into my local bank and explained what I had done to the loan officer. I took complete responsibility for my decisions and then asked her to loan me $25,000 as a debt consolidation loan for money that was stolen from me. I explained the whole situation and left nothing out of the story. The bank agreed to take a second note on my house and give me a four-year loan. When the paperwork was signed and I walked away from the bank, I had a payment of $653.10 per month to make on a debt that I would get nothing for. This was the money my broker had used to buy clothing, toys, goods and vacations.

As time went on, I was challenged with feelings of frustration, anger and bitterness, and so was my wife. But all along the way, I kept reminding myself and my wonderful wife that we had to let go of this experience and forgive, not holding anything back that would cause bitterness in our lives. We had to constantly remind ourselves that it was done and the debt no longer existed. Obviously, the bank didn't feel the same way because they expected their $653.10 promptly at the beginning of each month.

The decision I had made was to honor the biblical view of forgiveness and because of that, I believe that I reaped the biblical view of repentance. After talking with my wife that evening, I went for a walk and prayed. In my life, I have made a habit of giving to people in need and to organizations that help people both physically and spiritually as often as I can. I believe with every part of my being that we are meant to be givers. That night, I asked God to remember the giving I had done over the years. I asked Him to remember us while we were in financial difficulty. I didn't demand this of God; I asked humbly and with a grateful heart.

The next morning at 10:30 a.m., I got a call from my mother. She and my father had been up the night before and had been thinking and praying about what they should do with the small inheritance that she had gotten from my grandmother's estate. "Honey," she said, "Daddy and I kept thinking about you, and we want to give you $10,000 to help with your problem." Now, lest you think that this was just a sweet thing for them to do, you need to know that my parents were living at poverty level. They needed the money worse than anyone at that point, and yet, in their own hearts, they were convinced that they needed to give. Gratefully, I accepted, for in my family it would have been futile to have refused. Had I tried, my father would have just deposited the amount in my account on my behalf. Have I mentioned that they were also one of the six offended parties who were victimized by my broker?

After that, one at a time, opportunities came that manifested themselves in the form of extra cash. Not that I didn't have to work for it, because I did. But amazingly, these opportunities were not burdensome. At the end of every month, I would look at my business' profit and loss and there would be an additional $700.00. Like clockwork, the extra money would arrive—an extra computer hardware sale here, an extra programming project there. The visible effects of the loan on my family were negligible, and after my initial conversation with my wife, she never had an inkling that there was a bill to be paid. The payments simply happened.

Soon, I was approached by a prospective client that wanted a software package built from scratch. They refused to do it as a time and materials bid; it had to be fixed fee. Because I make more money on fixed fee, I was delighted that they held to their guns. And in a matter of fourteen months, all $25,000 had been paid off and I was back to ground zero again.

Since then, a number of years have passed and it's taken quite an amount of work on my part to convince my friend's family that I never blamed them for his actions. They were unsure of my sincerity because of the shame their son and brother had brought on their family name, but because I remained unchanged, they could see I was still the same old me. My relationship with his family is as good and perhaps even better now than it was before the whole mess happened. Believe it or not, I still call my ex-broker my friend. Does that mean I will sidestep common sense and deal with him in business? No. Trust and forgiveness are two different things altogether; the first is earned and the latter is given. I have lost trust in him, but his debt with me has been cancelled.

Just the other day, I was at a wedding and one of the other six offended parties was there. He approached me and said, "Hey, have you gotten any of your money back? He still owes my wife $9,000; he's driving around in a new sports car and we have gotten hardly anything at all." The frustration and bitterness was oozing out of his lips and eyes. I kindly looked at him and replied, "I'm well past that. It's not even on my mind." For the past number of years, I have continued to live a fabulous life free of frustration and bitterness toward my friend. This wedding guest chose not to forgive and has lived these last years constantly watching for his broker's repentance, embittered and angry at his friend, who became his thief. How much are years of frustration worth to you? How much would you pay to be freed from years of anger and bitterness? Freed from years of unmet expectations? I know what it was worth to me, and I'm glad I chose to forgive.

If you see yourself dealing with one or more situations that plague you, that rob your joy, that steal your thoughts, that anger and frustrate you when they touch even the lintel of your mind, consider the following:

1. Choose to forgive. Forgiveness is a choice that you must make. No one can make it for you. You have to reach down into the deepest caverns of your heart—down into the silent blackness—and determine to pull out every ounce of forgiveness that you can find. Biblical forgiveness is taught to us by Jesus Himself, and it says that if we want forgiveness, we must forgive in the exact same way. This is not just an emotional experience; it is a spiritual one as well. Ask God for help and expect Him to teach you how to forgive.

2. Choose to release. Releasing the debt that someone has created by their actions is the second step. You can say, "I'm not going to hold this wrong against them any further. I forgive it." But next you must say, "I'm not going to remember this debt anymore; I'm going to forget it." I'm not talking about repression; I'm talking about a willful decision to cast it to the wind and to treat that person as though the wrong never happened. Please know that I'm not suggesting that you lay all common sense aside and trudge right back into similar situations. I'm suggesting that you decide to go on with life and not be held back by the past.

3. Act on your forgiveness. In my case, I chose to write a letter releasing him from the debt and legally giving him the money he stole from me, and then I delivered that letter to him by hand. What can you do in your situation? What can you do that will

give feet to your intent? To say you forgive is one thing; to act upon that forgiveness is even more powerful. Just a caution at this point: when you act upon your forgiveness, you have to do it with no expectation from your offender. If you go in with the expectation that they will be grateful for your gift of grace and they spit in your face, you may walk away with a hurt that is ten times worse. Remember, we must offer forgiveness whether our offender is grateful for it or not. If he or she is incorrigible, you can walk away knowing that you have done everything in your power to bring reconciliation and you can be free from the mental, emotional and spiritual enslavement that you could have carried for years to come.

4. Don't talk. Your situation will become increasingly worse if you broadcast your pain to everyone you know. Natural human instinct is to spew words of frustration to anyone who will listen in an attempt to find sympathy and support. Doing this takes the wrong that was done and, by constant recitation, cements it in our hearts. This type of reaction only makes the process of forgiveness that much harder. Determine from the outset that you will not speak badly of your offender, and that if necessary, you won't speak of him at all. As I was going through this situation with my broker, I allowed only a small number of people in my life to know anything about what was happening. My wife, my pastor and a couple of very close friends were the only ones that I chose to trust and expose myself to. And even when I spoke with them about my situation, I watched my tongue so that I was not defaming my broker. Allow people to make mistakes gracefully if you can. Sometimes it's very difficult to do this, but I've always regretted the times when I haven't followed this guideline.

5. Fight your natural desire. Just like the aerodynamic law of lift, which takes a plane off the ground and sustains it in the air, supplants the law of gravity, there may be a law that applies to your case. I choose to look into the Bible for every major decision I make because every treasure of wisdom and knowledge

can be found in Jesus. I have never been ashamed of this fact or embarrassed by the outcome. I have experienced that the Bible presents the truth. Are there laws that, perhaps, go against your natural desire but may bring you more freedom? I challenge you to search diligently for them, apply them and watch for the outcome. Even if this is contrary to what you believe at this point in your life, I guarantee that it's worth any risk you may presume. Don't let the offense of Jesus' name and life stop you from pursuing the truth He brings. It is worth it to face whatever apprehensions and disbeliefs stand in the way.

6. Take responsibility for yourself. Chances are that you were part of the problem at some point along the way. Don't look at every situation as though you are an innocent bystander. While you may be innocent, carefully search your own involvement to see if you should bear any blame. In my case, I know that God warned me not to proceed, and had I listened, I would never have invested in the first place. I was responsible for my decision to continue on; no one forced me into it. Make a habit of taking responsibility for your part of the situation. Doing this makes you affirm that you are an imperfect person who can make mistakes. It also makes the forgiveness process easier. If you see where your making different decisions would have changed the outcome, it will relieve the "me versus them" attitude and make the forgiveness process a "we" process.

7. Never forget. How can I tell you to forgive but never to forget? Although at first this may sound confusing, it really shouldn't be. When you have walked through a situation that requires you to die a little—one that requires you to sacrifice your desire for vengeance so that you can extend the gift of forgiveness—never forget what brought you to that point. Was it selfishness? Was it greed? Was it pride? What was the root cause of your problem? Always remember this so that you don't make the same mistake twice. Why suffer the same problem all over again at a later date? Take heed not to forget. It may well save your life later.

EIGHT

SET YOUR MARGINS

Growing up in a home where my dad was making pretty good money working for a major corporation had its fine points. Dad worked hard during the week, and when the temperature was anywhere above 32 degrees Fahrenheit, we spent weekends and vacations at a beautiful lake, often swimming and snorkeling. I have many fond memories of lying in our camper at midnight and listening to the sound of the waves caressing the shore; of the curtains in the windows as the metal rings would tinkle against the rods from which they hung while being whisked about by the passing breeze. At first dawn, dad would get out his propane stove and cook fresh side—thick bacon that had not been cured. Even as I'm writing this, I feel like one of Pavlov's dogs. We would eat breakfast and then nuzzle into our lake chairs, watching the sunlight dance on the lake and resting in the simplicity of book reading, often dozing off with the wind whispering in our ears.

> I find that being a husband and a parent is an extremely uncomfortable job for which I feel desperately unprepared.

When we next woke up, it was time for lunch—usually a sandwich, chips and a black cherry soda. And then, after staying out of the water for forty-five minutes, lest we should get the infamous leg cramps, we'd go and exhaust ourselves in the lake as we journeyed around on our inner tubes and air mattresses. But my favorite part was just after we would eat supper: we would get back in those wonderful lake chairs and enshroud ourselves with as many blankets as we needed to stay warm, sometimes sitting close together to merge our body heat, and we would drink coffee, eat Russian peanuts and watch the moon scale across the nighttime sky.

All these vignettes may sound rather simplistic to you, but they are among some of my fondest memories. I hope that you can sit and recall similar stories with your family. But even with these fulfilling childhood memories, there was a great price that was paid. I never remember my dad being home without a lapboard, an adding machine and a stack of papers from his office. I have few memories of my dad and I just going out to throw a baseball or a Frisbee. His evenings were usually consumed with work, and it didn't leave much time for anything else. On top of that, his and my relationship was very poor all the way through my adolescent and teenage years. I had the uncanny ability to push his anger button and to set him off. What is even more fascinating is that between my nineteenth and twenty-first birthdays, my dad became a very wise man and from that time to now, God has granted me a wonderful relationship with him for which I'm very grateful.

The truth that has bewildered me for quite some time is that I have followed some of the same life patterns that I saw and disapproved of in my dad. It takes everything within me not to fall into the same pits he did. And, not only that, it is now my sixty-five-year-old father who tells me, "Son, you'd better slow down. Don't do what I did."

I have discovered that as I am getting older, my responsibility and my load continues to increase: this load is comprised of my work responsibilities, my relationship with my wife, my relationship with my son, my relationship with my daughter, my relationships with my friends, my relationships with my clients, my business management responsibilities, my family's safety, my personal devotional time and as my and my wife's parents are aging, my concerns for their health, wellness and finances. These cares can all be very daunting to say the least.

My work world is one in which I deal with facts, figures, politics, people and problems. Over and again, I work to keep businesses running and to help them work through their difficulties so that they can make more money at what they do. This is a very left-brained, logic-minded lifestyle. I spend nine to ten hours in this mode of thought and from here I then leap through the front door of my home and am expected to immediately set aside my day, retire the logical left half of my brain and attempt to give my family my undivided creative, right-brained attention so that I can make a dog out of modeling clay.

I find that being a husband and a parent is an extremely uncomfortable job for which I feel desperately unprepared at the end of my professional day. Some evenings, I have a horrible time letting go so that I can be what my wife and kids need me to be. I find that work is a less sensitive place, generally void of unspoken personal expectations that only family can hold. At work there are rules governing your position and others' expectations toward you. At work there is no expectation on you to burst out into childish frolicking. This is not so with home life, and it's an excellent thing that the two are not similar in nature. You see, whether you are married—whether you have children—there has to be a time and place when you come home, let down your hair and act juvenile. If you don't, you will maintain the stressors of your day, and you will fly off the handle at every little thing that happens—whether it's cursing at the can opener for not working properly, or yelling at your nine-year-old for accidentally spilling her water glass onto the carpet.

The older I get, the more familiar I become with my professional world, and the more comfortable I become living there. Because I spend 200 percent more of my waking time in my job culture, I find that unless I proactively push against the walls that are closing in on me—unless I refuse to be sucked in to the familiar—I, too, will be compacted into a tiny cube known as a workaholic, and when my life is done, I will be lying on my deathbed wondering why my children, wife and family aren't beside me as I pass from this life into eternity.

I have discovered why men and women end up having affairs in the workplace. It's not necessarily because they are unhappy at home but because the black hole of familiarity continues to suck them in. I have come to realize why people have heart attacks as they are sitting in their offices at 9:20 p.m. on a Thursday night; it's not because they have nothing else to do but because they have vanished into the Bermuda Triangle of familiarity. What gives our workaday world such a strong and familiar hold on our lives? It's because of missing margins.

What value do margins add? I'm sure you can remember. Journey back. Look through your mind's eye all the way back to fourth grade. Your teacher says, "Children, we are going to the library, and you may choose any book you wish on which to write a report." You anxiously start pulling books off the shelf. In less than three seconds you can tell if the book in your hand is worthy of writing a report. Your speed and ability to ingest an entire book's contents is dumbfounding. You are phenomenal at choosing the perfect book with a wonderful story line and meaningful literary characters. What are you looking for in the perfect read? Big print and wide margins! Even in fourth grade, you understand that the larger the print and the wider the margins, the less work you have to do to get the job done and get the credit you need. No one needs to teach you this—it is intrinsic to your makeup as a member of humanity. Certainly, I'm not suggesting that we maintain an attitude of laziness in our workplace, but somewhere in the course of our human journey, we try to stuff more and more on a page. We make the print smaller and smaller. And then, one day, we decide to get rid of that wasted space on the sides, top and bottom until all we have left is one continuous line of text snaking from the far upper-left corner of the page all the way down to the furthest bottom-right pica.

We've lost sight of the fact that it is soothing to the eyes when we read a book with margins; that our eyes applaud us when we read a page where the print is something more than six-point pitch. Let me enumerate some of the margin and pitch setters that I have established in my life. If they are applicable to you, perhaps you can consider setting them for yourself as well.

Determine when your day is done. If you are married, talk with your spouse about this. Decide that at a given time each day, you are going to walk away from your responsibilities and leave them lying in your basket and voice-mail box at work. In my case, I don't do anything past 6:30 p.m. unless my family is involved. I allow myself a few days each month to splurge and stay past that time, but it is not a common occurrence. I used to volunteer my time as a member of a private school board. We would have meeting after meeting, and the meetings would go until 11:00 p.m. and sometimes later. It was a very rewarding experience because we were touching the lives of a number of children. But when my three-year term was complete, I swore I'd never do it again while my children were living at home because it took too much of a toll on my family. What sense is there in investing my whole life in other people's children if I am sacrificing mine in the process?

If you are an unmarried person, your margins may be different, but I suggest that you focus on the freedoms you have waiting for you at home. You'll find that you have more time to enjoy your friends, read a good book or rejuvenate yourself from a hectic day.

Watch for familiarity pitfalls with your coworkers. Close working relationships and familiarity breed a commonality that can be destructive if you're married. This type of closeness may lead you into an improper relationship that could cause you to hurt the people you love the most in your life. I don't know any married person who woke up one morning and said, "I think today is the day I'll stop loving my spouse and children! Darn it! I'm going to go to work and find someone with whom to have an affair." I would intimate that it usually happens due to lack of margins.

Personally, my margins are wide in this area. First, I never take business trips with anyone of the opposite gender. I won't travel out of town in a car with someone of the opposite gender unless there is a group of male and female travelers in the same vehicle. If it is just one woman, I excuse myself and drive in my own vehicle. There have been a few times that I've suffered ridicule for this margin, but I love my wife and children enough to avoid extending myself past what I consider to be the proper realm of familiarity. I have explained to business associates that I believe strongly in avoiding "even the appearance of evil," and when I do so, my conviction is generally accepted and sometimes applauded.

Second, when I'm traveling in town to a luncheon and it becomes necessary to drive with someone of the opposite sex, I wait until I'm in the car with my business associate, and then I call my wife to tell her who I'm with and where we're going. I do this for two reasons. First, it communicates publicly that I'm married and that my wife knows who I'm with. Secondly, if anyone ever comes to my spouse and says, "Hey, I saw your husband with another woman," she is already aware of the situation and it doesn't put her in a sensitive position.

Finally, if you find yourself being drawn to someone at work—if you are becoming more familiar with them, if you are beginning to feel a close attachment or drawing to them, if you see that your margin is thinning—go to your spouse and talk about it. Let him or her know that you aren't interested in your coworker, and it is because of your commitment to your spouse that you are exposing this "familiar" situation. Ask God for wisdom on how to handle this, and ask your spouse to hold you accountable. Pray together about it if you can—doing this adds another layer of commitment to each other. There will be a sting to this at first, but if you have a solid marriage, it should strengthen your relationship in the long run because your spouse will know that if you are ever in this type of situation again, you will come to him or her and expose it.

If you fear that your relationship with your spouse isn't solid enough to handle this kind of confession right now, find someone of the same gender who you can trust and who will hold you accountable. Whatever you do, lay down the guidelines for your margin and hold on to them—even at the risk of hurting or offending your coworker.

Here are some tips for adding margins to your daily life:

1. Start adding margins before going home. Consider taking a meandering walk at your local mall; running by the park and sitting on the hood of your car; going by the Y and exercising; taking a different route home and driving slowly to enjoy the trip. Do whatever it takes to break the cycle of your workday before you walk in the door of your home. This is an important thing to do whether you have family waiting at home for you or not. It makes you more ready to relax and remember that home is your safe haven.

2. Take time to recognize God at the beginning of your day. I can only tell you that the difference in my day is absolute when I start it off with prayer and a time digesting the Truth found in my Bible. It gives me the opportunity to keep my focus on what is most important in my life and to allow God's Holy Spirit the chance to show me if there's anything I've done wrong and need to correct before the day begins. This time is priceless and has saved me innumerable headaches over the course of my life. Because this is the most valuable margin, it also seems to be the hardest margin to maintain.

3. Let your voicemail pick up the business calls after 6:30 p.m. Just because you have a phone doesn't mean that you have to answer it. It is there to serve you, not for you to serve it. Also, by screening your calls, you are the one who chooses whether the call is of such grave importance that you have to give up your personal time to take care of it. If it's absolutely necessary, do it. But if not, don't let that margin decrease. The call will be there tomorrow.

4. Stop working. Make a habit of taking a break in the morning and in the afternoon and of eating lunch away from your desk. This is a foreign consideration to a number of people, but the fact is, you generally don't feel yourself getting stressed while it is happening. It's only after you break the cycle and get away from the stressors that you realize that you are tense. A couple of fifteen-minute hiatuses along with a real lunch break on a daily basis will reduce the stress before it builds.

As for me, my wakeup call on this missing margin came one afternoon about 2:30 p.m. I was on client site working hard. In the months preceding, I had just installed a ten-city-wide area network, written the software that the corporation was using to track half its $50 million revenues, and I was single-handedly managing their information technology department. I had support calls out my ears, bug fixes to software I had written and the list went on. All of a sudden, my heart skipped three or four beats in a row, I got dizzy and my eyesight started to blur. I leaned back in my chair and thought, "I'm having a heart attack." After about five minutes, I was at least able to stand up, but I was still quite shaken. I went to the on-campus nurse and had her take my blood pressure. It was 132 over 95, which for me was a huge change. My normal resting blood pressure is 106 over 63. I was about thirty points higher on both sides. It was at that point that I realized I needed to change.

Whatever the case, do something and don't wait until you're on a hospital bed with tubes coming out of you to decide to de-stress on a regular basis. Those little breaks will make a world of difference in your tension level and will greatly enhance your overall quality of life. By getting up every couple of hours to walk around, you'll notice a decrease in back, shoulder and neck pain. If you suffer from headaches, you may discover that they decrease or vanish all together.

NINE

LIVE BENEATH YOUR MEANS

This topic could have been covered in the chapter on setting margins, but because it is so multi-faceted, it seems appropriate to deal with it separately. Time and time again people rack up debt until they can't find a way out of it. We live in an economic society where there is so much offered to so many people so much of the time that we end up so far in debt that we can't find a way out. School loans, car loans, house loans, RV loans, boat loans, debt consolidation loans, gas cards, phone cards and credit cards constitute the norm for people's financial status today. On top of that, we want everything *now*. We are a drive-through society where if it is appealing to our eyes and we think life would be better with it, we buy it and worry about how to pay for it later.

At the age of fourteen, I was excited about buying my first car. Despite what I wanted, my parents decided I needed a Chevy Citation. I think they figured that if I drove a family car, I wouldn't get into any trouble. Through a series of events, I ended up losing the car before I had paid it off. I spent five months paying for a car I didn't have because I financed it for way longer than I needed to and didn't pay it off soon enough. It was at this point that I learned the shorter the term of a loan, the better off you are on your purchase because you never know what will happen later in life.

With that lesson in mind, I continued on as a wiser individual. Time flew by and I was finally out of college. I badly needed a car. I was driving a boat—a 1977 Chevy Malibu. It was a blast to drive, but it was a little unsightly. It was puke green with one royal blue fender that I had replaced myself, and which I had gotten from the junkyard. I drove to a local car dealership and parked on the lot. Now, I have to confess at this point that I love shopping for cars. Some people love to play football because it's a full-contact, highly competitive sport. Others enjoy basketball because of the type of skill that's involved with landing a three-point shot; for me, it's car buying. Although I've never experienced it as a full-contact sport, this particular occurrence was as close as it could get.

I parked my beaut of a car and started to walk around the lot. After a few moments, I found the car of my dreams: a 1993 Honda Prelude. It was candy-apple red with a sunroof, a moonroof and four-wheel steering. It was everything that I had wanted in a car. It was also quite a bit more than I could afford. The asking price was $9,800, but man, what a car.

Now, lest you misunderstand the rest of this account, you have to realize that I believe strongly in living beneath my means. The reasons for this will be given later. But suffice it to say that when I walk on a car lot, I know how much I can afford, and it's substantially less than the average person. I don't waiver from what I have in recognizable cash. So, when I saw that car, I knew it was considerably more than I had, but I was determined to make it mine nonetheless.

When I was finally approached by a sales person, I explained that I had $5,200 that I could spend on a car—I knew I could afford payments on that amount for three years and not put myself in a crunch financially. The sales person looked at me and said, "There's no way the manager will even consider that price. How much can you afford each month?" That question is the torpedo that sinks the submarine of financial freedom for almost every person I know. When you begin looking at objects in terms of payments rather than the total amount you can afford, you begin the freefall into the abyss of debt. I'm not saying that payments are bad, but if you only look at a payment, you lose sight of the larger picture: the total cost!

I explained to the salesman that I don't price things based on payments and that I had $5,200 to spend on an automobile. He retorted with, "I understand that, but how much can you afford each month for a car payment?" Again, I had to underscore that I would not purchase a car in that manner. Finally I said, "Your job isn't to tell me what your sales manager will accept, it is to represent me and present my offer. Now, please go tell him I'll give $5,200 for this car." Well, that set the tone for the next two-and-a-half hours. By the end of the whole experience, I was amazed that they were still playing cat and mouse with me. I had never wavered from the position that all I had was $5,200, but they tried to get me to finance it for five years and to go up in price. And the tricks and attempts didn't stop there.

By the time this experience came to a close, I was pinned in a corner of the sales manager's office. In the room with me were my salesman, the lead salesman and the sales manager, all standing around me in a quasi-triangle. At this point, these words fell out of the sales manager's mouth, "Okay. The lot owner has agreed to sell you the car for $5,300. You can pay that can't you? After all, it's only $100." My reply was, "If it means so little to you, just take it off the price of the car." With that, the three got up, told me that they would take this to the owner of the lot and be back with me shortly. I waited for another fifteen minutes, and after no one came back into the office, I decided that the game was over. I picked up my coat, casually walked over to my vehicle, got in and began motoring off the lot. The salesman sprinted out to my car in an attempt to salvage the sale, and that's when it very nearly became a full-contact sport.

Now, those of you who are in car sales are probably cursing at me right now because you think I was wasting that sales person's time.

But, in truth, it was the buyer who lost that time, not just the sales person. I had been truthful and up front from the very beginning. Admittedly, this experience was steeped in immaturity, but it does make a point. A behemoth problem in the realm of commissioned sales is that the sales person isn't used to dealing with people in a straightforward fashion. Everything is based on how big of a sale can be made. There is little-to-no concern about the ongoing welfare of the man or woman who buys the product on a payment plan, and most salespeople are ill-prepared to deal with cash sales on expensive items. From the salesperson's perspective, as long as the sale is just enough to make the buyer wince, and as long as the commission check is paid, life is good. After all, he is trying to make a living, and everyone in business works to find that same spot—where the price is as high as it can go without losing business. You can't blame them. But, as the buyer, if you know this ahead of time, you don't have to give in to it.

What would our society be like if everyone stuck unwaveringly to financial convictions such as this? We might be living in smaller homes that we could afford in ten years instead of thirty. Certainly, a small home has its benefits because there's not as much to clean and not as much to maintain. We would be driving cars that weren't nearly as fancy. They probably wouldn't cost as much to maintain or to drive, and then we could pay the car off in a year instead of five. In some cases, we might even be able to keep one parent home. Gee, we might even have money to give to others. I know that seems a bit cynical, but how many people do you know who purposely live beneath their means so that they can give the rest away?

Let me stop at this point to say that if you are a single parent, please don't take offense at this. I have deep respect for you, and I feel for you. I have seen how difficult it is to make a living, take care of your children, raise them without a spouse and try to keep your sanity. But, in living beneath your means, you must also let people into your life to help you out. There are people who can help with your children, your home repairs and even your auto repairs if they just know there is a need. Don't be afraid to ask for assistance. There's nothing wrong with doing this, and it gives people a chance to do something outside themselves that will make them feel better about who they are and what they bring to the community.

What is wrong with making our goal to live off 10 percent of our income and to give 90 percent of it away? Why can't we make that the socioeconomic dream? I have decided that no matter how well my business is doing, I will still take the same basic amount home month after month. Even in years that I've made a six-figure income, I've still operated my household expenses with almost the same amount as I did back in 1995. What has that accomplished in my life? All the residual income that was left over was used to give and to pay off previous debt. I have no credit card debt; I do use them for purchases, but they get paid off every month. I have a house that I paid off in seven years instead of thirty. My latest car purchase was done knowing where the cash was coming from and was paid off in less than a year. We pay to put our children through private school because it is important to us. And on top of all of this, we still have fun vacations together and money to give away.

By living beneath our means, we have not stopped ourselves from having a wonderful life and enjoying nice things. Instead, we enjoy a better life because we don't have to work overtime to pay interest; we don't have to work two jobs to make ends meet. It's very freeing not to have a lot of debt. Currently, we give about 22 percent of our income to organizations that we believe are necessary for the health and wellness of people, both physically and spiritually. I offer you a challenge. Will you go against the tide of self-centered capitalism and care enough about others to do the same thing? What will it take in your life to get you out of debt so that you can be free to find and give to those people and organizations that are important to you?

If you want to live beneath your means, here are some hints that may help:

1. Destroy the cards. If you can't use credit cards effectively, then cut them into pieces and throw them away. Credit card debt is a gigantic problem, and it is very difficult to get out of it once you are in it. If you have as little as $1,000 worth of credit card debt, you will pay almost $360 in interest over the course of a year if you let it go. Don't fall prey to this carnivorous process. Do what it takes to rid yourself of the temptation.

2. Don't ever buy things based on time. Get into your head a total dollar amount that you can spend and stick to it no matter what. When you purchase any big-ticket item, don't ever look at the cost as a matter of payments. You will lose every time. When you need a new refrigerator, see how much you can afford. You don't need an ice maker, a water dispenser, a beer tap and music when the door opens. If all you can afford with cash is a rectangular box with shelves and refrigerant, then make that your purchase and be happy that you have a fridge. Then, save up your money over the next few years and replace it when you have the money together.

   If you don't have any cash, you absolutely need a refrigerator and there is no way around financing it, look at your budget and see how much of a payment you can afford in six months or less. Multiply that amount by the number of months, six or less, and use that amount to buy your fridge. Don't look at financing it for two or three years. You are only looking at difficulties down the road.

3. When it comes to cars, don't be afraid to wait and shop around. And don't get sucked into buying something on payments that are spread over sixty months. That is a gargantuan amount of time. To keep it in perspective, sixty months is the same amount of time that passed in your life from eighth grade until you started your freshman year in college. Think about installment purchases in this fashion and keep perspective.

   If you absolutely have to buy a car on time, then figure how much you can afford for twelve or twenty-four months and buy something at that level. Don't believe your sales person when he shows you his first choice at your asking price. Many will often start showing you something that is junky to make you want to spend more—to condition you for something more expensive. Just hold to your guns. Even if it means walking away and coming back repetitively, saying the same thing every time: "I only have $X to spend. Has anything come in yet?" Stay consistent and your efforts will pay off. But just remember, once you buy into the lie about payment based purchases, it's very hard to retrain your mind to think on cash basis again.

4. Start giving. In the book of Proverbs 19:17, the Bible says, "He who gives to the poor lends to the Lord and He will not forget what was done." Don't wait until you can "afford" to give, start to give now—even if it's five or ten dollars. Make a regular habit of giving to people who you know are poor or to organizations that deal with the poor. There is such a huge need in your own neighborhood for help. If everyone reading this book would give $10 a month to help feed and clothe the poor, it could make a major impact.

Giving does a number of things, but most importantly, I believe it gets our eyes off of ourselves and places them on others. This brings health to our souls and brings the focus of our lives down to a palatable experience. When you give, you feel better about yourself and you honor God. There is just no way to describe the feeling of joy that I get when I give money to people or organizations that I know need it. At Christmas, I am aware of people's great need and always make a habit of giving money to families in need. I do it anonymously, and to my knowledge, none of the families has ever found out who has given to them. But, hearing of their excitement when they get the gifts is priceless.

Personally, I remember one stark Christmas when all I had to eat was rice and chicken soup for supper and peanut butter and jelly sandwiches for lunch. I had no money for anything else, and that is what I ate for two months straight. One day, a lady from my church came to me and said, "I was praying this morning, and I knew in my heart that I was to clean out my cupboards and give you everything that I had." Man, did I have a feast that night. At that point, there was nothing more enjoyable or pleasing to me than a couple cans of peas, some green beans and spaghetti. I say this to convey that whatever you do will have benefits for the recipient—even if it's just a can of green beans and some spaghetti.

5. Don't be ashamed of how you live. No matter what type of home, what type of car or what types of toys you have, don't be ashamed. Don't let status, position or fear of others drive you into purchases. If you choose to live beneath your means and that forces you to live in a trailer, don't be ashamed. If you have to buy a car that is $500—you know, a real beater—don't be ashamed. Even if you are a doctor and you have $120,000 in school bills to pay off, don't be afraid to live in a 900-square-foot house. You are setting the pattern now so that your life will be better down the line. I'm convinced that if we just work through the first few years of denying ourselves the things we want immediately, we will see our desires fulfilled later on down the line once we have learned how to be good stewards over our finances. We must simply take it one step at a time and choose to not compare ourselves to others.

6. Don't give up. After you have worked at mastering this law for a while, you will probably grow tired of not having the things you want. I didn't realize how addictive buying things can be. I think it's like smoking or any other vice you may be familiar with. For me, I had gone for a while without anything, and I was doing really well. I was working at a local upscale department store, and I would see everyone wearing amazing clothes. I had nothing stylish to speak of and was hungry for the self-attention. So, I applied for a credit account at the store and went out to try on the best jeans and shirts I could find. I felt so good in my new duds that I even wore one of those

pairs of jeans the rest of that day. In a matter of an hour, I had racked up a $300 credit card bill. At the time I was only making $5.00 an hour so that was about sixty hours worth of work just to pay off the principal, not to mention any interest that would accrue. But, all that mattered was that I looked sweet and I felt great about myself...until two days later. All of a sudden, I looked at myself in the mirror and came to my senses. I couldn't believe what I had done. I had set all self-control aside and lavished myself with what felt good.

In a panicked frenzy, I loaded it all up: shirts, pants and all and took it back to the store. I returned every piece of clothing. It doesn't end there. When I came to work the next day, I was called into the operations manager's office. As I walked into his office, there on the chair in front of me were all the pants and shirts I had purchased a few days before. I was invited to take a seat, and as I sat there, my hands shook as I processed my fear and utter shame. My manager corrected me and explained how disappointed he was that I would do such a thing. I swore to him that I had only worn one pair of those jeans and that the rest had been untouched. But he wouldn't believe me. Why should he? I had proven myself untrustworthy. By the time the conversation was done, he held me to bar for the pair that I had confessed to wearing, and he released me from the rest of the debt—except for the weighty debt of proving my trustworthiness all over again.

When you feel like you've had enough and you just want to go out and blow money on yourself in a spending frenzy, realize that it's a passing phase and you will reap the rewards of abstinence just a little further in your journey. If you've done well, grant yourself a reward like a new shirt or blouse—just do it on clearance and don't give in to the temptation to spend your way into the caverns of debt. You'll see that delaying your gratification really is worth it once you have paddled for a while on the river Freedom and are able to see that you have no debt tying you to the dock. Cut the cord and make the trip; the exercise will do you good.

TEN

SPEND TIME TO MAKE MONEY OR MONEY TO MAKE TIME

In the capitalist world where we live, no matter your station in life, your financial bracket or poverty level, there is a law that affects your daily life whether you realize it or not. If there was ever anything that has frustrated me more in life personally and professionally, it is this rule, and you will do well to memorize it. Write it on the sun visor of your car if necessary, but don't let it out of your sight: you either spend time to make money or you spend money to make time.

To explain what I mean, I will approach this truth from two different angles: a facts and figures angle and then a more down-to-earth angle. If one doesn't make sense, keep reading, and hopefully the other will.

Imagine that it's 6:30 p.m. and you are still at work. Your friends are meeting at the Y for an evening game of basketball. You have another thirty minutes of work to go, and then you still have to drive thirty minutes to get to the game. You know that if you work that last thirty minutes, there is no way you'll be able to enjoy the game because by the time you get to the Y, the teams will have been chosen and the game will be over a third of the way done. How much is that extra thirty minutes of work worth to you? Stop for a minute and calculate it.

Let's say you make $60.00 per hour. That means that every half hour you work will yield you $30.00. If you are making $60.00 per hour, that also means you are paying at least 28 percent for your income taxes and other types of withholding. That drops your profit down to $21.60 for the half hour. Now, because your game would have gone from 7:00 p.m. to 8:30 p.m., you've actually lost an hour and a half of relaxation, friendship and exercise. If you take that $21.60 (which you probably blow in one night of eating out) and you divide it by the 1.5 hours of enjoyment you would have had, it comes out to $14.40 per hour. So the question before the board is this: is it worth $14.40 per hour to miss out on your relaxation, recreation and exercise just so you can stay at work, be stressed and then go home, sit in front of the TV and try to unwind with a TV dinner? If you want to look at it differently, would it be worth $14.40 per hour to get away from the office and to end your day with your friends?

Now, if you only make $18.00 per hour, the numbers fall like this: $18.00 at an 18 percent tax bracket makes a net of $7.38 for a half hour worth of pay. You work that extra half hour and you make enough to eat fast food for lunch the next day. But, given that you will lose that same 1.5 hours of enjoyment by staying late at the office, is it worth $4.92 per hour to quit working for the day and enjoy some exercise and relaxation with your friends?

If these illustrations don't click, how about this down-to-earth example from my own household. My wife is a diligent homemaker. When my children were born, she made the decision to stay home with them, and because we lived beneath our means, we were able to do it. However, she has the most difficult time spending money. It drives her to tears if she has to spend retail price for something that she wants. As a matter of fact, she simply won't do it.

Recently, she began remodeling our basement. After working a couple of weeks, she decided that she wanted to place some curtains downstairs. That started a conversation between the two of us about the cost of curtains. So that she wouldn't have to spend much money, she had decided to buy some eggplant-colored, rectangular tablecloths that she found on clearance and then find some way to make a loop at the long end of them so that she could slide them over a wooden dowel rod that she would affix to the ceiling. After discussing the ways she could do it, she decided she wanted to get some fabric glue to make the rod pocket since her sewing skills are…well, anyway.

Knowing the way things work in my home, I brought up the possibility that she might use that fabric glue on the tablecloth, roll the edge of the table cloth over to make that one-inch trough through which the dowel rod would pass, and then realize that it should have been a two-inch trough. I asked her if she had considered buying these wonderful little curtain hooks that have loops on one end and clasping teeth on the other to hold the fabric. She looked at me and said, "I couldn't spend that much; they are $6 for a set of four, and I would need three sets." She further informed me that she would be spending more on the curtain rings than she did on the tablecloths to make the curtains, and she just couldn't make herself do it.

I explained to her that time is worth money, and that if it didn't work with the fabric glue, the tablecloths would have to be repurchased. I then threw out the fact that after making a trough on one end, she could never reuse those tablecloths for anything but curtains. It was then that she realized it would be cheaper to spend the extra $18.00 to buy the hooks than to try and jury-rig the curtains and save a few bucks.

Here, then, is the point. You have to get past simple thoughts like, "If I work, I can make an extra $30.00." Or, "I can't spend that extra $18.00, I'll just have to make this work." If that same amount of time was spent doing something else, what would the outcome of that other activity be worth to you? What would you pay to do it or to have it done? What would you pay for the time to sit down and read a book?

What would you pay for the time to go and clean one of your kid's rooms or to clean your garage? Is it worth losing half an hour of pay so that you can have an hour and a half of recreation with your friends? Is it worth paying a little extra so that your duties go more quickly and you can move past the necessary and into the desired? Certainly if we spend all our time doing everything we have to do, then we never have time to do the things we want. How much is it worth to begin experiencing the things you want? Factor these unmet desires into the cost of what you are doing or buying. The time, the activity, the item may have

> **How much is it worth to begin experiencing the things you want?**

more value to you than the money you could have made or saved. You can't just evaluate things at face value; you have to factor in cost, savings, time lost and time gained. Remember, you spend time to make money or money to make time.

The Hispanic culture has always amazed me. I believe we have a lot to learn from this culture. In my travels down to old Mexico, I'm always bewildered by the amount of together-time people spend with one another. At 11:00 p.m., children are out during non-school months playing stickball under a streetlight. Families are sitting in their front lawns by mid-afternoon enjoying the shade and each other's company. To have all this time together, what do they pay? Money. They spend time together until 11:00 p.m. instead of working at the office until 11:00 p.m. and leaving their family and friends as a sacrifice on the altar of materialism.

If you are someone who works twelve hours a day, why do you do it? What are you buying? You're earning money by working, but where is it going? Are you investing it in a retirement fund that you may never get to use because you don't take care of yourself, you eat poorly and have no time for exercise? Are you investing it for strangers who will take it when you are gone? Strangers who you were married to or people to whom you gave life? What value is there in this type of existence? You work your fingers to the bone and in the end you lose all that is dear. Of all the clergy I have ever dealt with, of all the funerals I have attended, of all the EMTs I've had this discussion with and of all the final phone calls that I have ever heard coming from catastrophic situations, I have never heard anyone's last words as anything but, "I love you. Tell the kids I love them. I'm sorry if I've ever hurt you." When will you have your last conversation? Will the last words you utter in this life be a curse over the work you try so hard to perform? Or will you live out your final words by deciding to spend money to make time and then investing that time in those who really matter?

Right now, you may be thinking, "If I do that, I may get fired!" Perhaps it's time to find a new job where your employer is more in-line with your priorities. How much is your free time worth? How much is time worth to you in general? How much are the objects and experiences that take up your time worth now?

As you begin to answer these questions for yourself, let me offer some thoughts:

1. Figure out your real wage. Do an honest assessment of how much you actually clear from your job. See how much your pay is for every hour you work. Take out taxes, health benefits and everything else that decreases your pay and work your way down to an amount representing the actual take-home pay you get to keep. If you are a stay-at-home parent, figure your hourly wage at one half of your spouse's wages—you're worth more than that, but you must start somewhere. Memorize that dollar amount and then when you have to make decisions about whether you're going to leave work and do something or stay there and earn your income, you will have already done the math.

2. Think outside the box. If your employer expects you to work forty-five hours as a salaried employee and it's taking you sixty hours to do your work, talk to your boss. Explain your situation, ask for a day to get away and then go through everything you are responsible for. This isn't a vacation day. It's a workday.

Examine your job duties from top to bottom. If you don't know why you are doing something, ask. There have been numerous times when I have found work being done at a company that no longer needed to be done. Perhaps there was a need for information twenty years ago that no longer exists, but because people never realized the information wasn't necessary anymore, it is still being generated and disseminated. Over and again I've found that when all the work is done, no one does anything with the outcome but file it. Those things can often be nixed, or created quarterly or annually instead. When you are done, lay out a plan to restructure your day, your work habits or your surroundings so that you aren't taking a 25 percent pay cut for working that extra fifteen hours.

After doing all of this, if you literally have sixty hours worth of work each week, humbly approach your supervisor and discuss it with him. Chances are that if you have a human as a supervisor, he will be sympathetic and try to help you work it out. If you don't have a human for a supervisor, the decision is yours as to how important your free time really is to you.

3. Find what can be delegated, and delegate it. If you have direct reports whose workload you can influence and you are able to teach them to take a portion of your workload for you, do it. If you can spread that extra work out among three or four employees, you've just saved yourself the load, you've helped them increase their knowledge of your job and you've made them more valuable to the organization as a whole.

4. Don't just look at face value. It doesn't matter if you are a homemaker, a student or a corporate president; don't assume that the face value of something is all that it actually costs. You have what is known as opportunity cost as well. By saving the money you see at face value, what do you lose? Do you lose time? Do you lose freedom? Do you lose relationships? What is the value beyond what you can see? Be certain that you add those items to the cost, and don't leave them out of your decision.

5. Realize where your real wealth lies. If you were on your death-bed and you had fifteen seconds to say anything to anyone, what would your final words be? Stop reading right now and think about this for just a few moments. Imagine yourself lying on the pavement after a disastrous car crash. Who would you want to see? What would you want to say? How would you feel if you knew you could never get the words out? Where would you rather be? Once you've gotten that into your head, take fifteen seconds and see if you can fit it all in. If you can't, then begin taking steps to make yourself available to those people in those places to say the things that you just thought of. Remind yourself that this could really happen to you. It can happen to any of us at any time. And if it's not you, it could happen to the people you want to be around. What if it was your spouse, your child, your friend or your parent who never had the op-portunity to say those final words to you because you were never there or because when you were there, you were always distant, your mind held captive by the living you made? What would you pay then? Would you pay that time with your fam-ily and friends to continue making money? Or, would you pay any amount of money you had to get that time back?

It seems that there is a hierarchy in our lives. When we are well we seldom think about sickness, and when we are sick, we can think of nothing but being well. When you are well, how much time will you spend to make money? When you are sick, how much money will you spend to make time? Check yourself. Is it backward?

ELEVEN

FREEDOM IS WORTH MORE THAN MONEY

How many times have you peered outside your office window (if you're lucky enough to have one), seen the golden sun streaking through an angelically blue sky, felt its warmth radiating through the pane of glass and murmured to yourself, *Boy, I wish I could be outside*? Unfortunately, the American business culture is so profit-driven that it has completely shut out life and life has shut it out. The corporate employee is trapped inside this runaway car with little means of escape. Who decided that it is wrong to have a two-hour lunch break? Why is it wrong to take the afternoon off when it's sunny outside so that you can enjoy it? What is wrong with sleeping in once in a while so that you can placate your weary soul with your down-filled comforter for another hour? It seems to me that given the benefits of doing such things, these should be the rule rather than the exception; the enjoyment of such experiences would bring reduced stress and more joy to life. But, we are dealing with an economy where businesses are so focused, so nearsighted when it comes to making money that they fail to see that freedom is worth more than money—not only to themselves but to all of those who they employ.

As a business owner, I have had a lot of fun with my employees as I exposed them to freedom in the workplace. I've enjoyed letting my employees work from home. With the proper controls, it's really not a bad fit. I've called employees at home early in the morning and said, "Hey, you know, it's supposed to be beautiful out today. Why don't you take the day off and spend it with your spouse?" After doing that to one employee, I had to argue with him because he couldn't believe I was being truthful with him. But, after some insistence, he finally relented and realized that I was indeed serious and was honoring him with such a gift. I've contacted the accounting department and asked them to cut checks for $50.00 and to hand them out to my employees at a later time. I then made a conference call to my staff and told them the following, "You will get a check in just a few moments. Your only responsibility is to take the check and spend all of it on yourself. You may have the rest of the day to do it; however, you must spend it all, you must spend it all on *yourself* and none of it can remain by 5:00 p.m." Again, people were amazed and couldn't believe it. After all, who would give them money and then pay for their afternoon of shopping? I believe so strongly in my employees that I did just that. Even after doing these things, I still managed to bring home a nice income, and the reward of honoring my employees with such freedoms was enormous.

Possibly one of the reasons we have become so stringent regarding our work policies is because at some time in the past we have been taken advantage of or perhaps even stolen from. But, we can't allow the abuse of freedoms or finances to bring us to the point where we have such strict and heartless demands on others that it becomes a prison for our workers. When groups of people must work together, I realize that we need rules such as, "no loud music" and "no burning candles at your desk," but freedom goes much farther than that. It goes into the world of each individual person and what they see as most valuable in their scope of life. One person may value free time in the morning that he can replace at the end of his work day. Another may want to work at home in the comfort of his pajamas and near his own coffee pot. Still another may see freedom as the ability to run around on her lunch hour and not be scolded if she comes back twenty minutes later than she is expected. It all comes down to trust, and I would intimate that our businesses are run more out of fear than out of freedom.

What would happen if every employee we maintained took as much pride and ownership in our business as we, the owners and directors, did? What would happen if people in your accounts receivable department cared as much about your receivables as the owners of the business? What about the sales people, the line staff, the nurses, the maintenance people? I guarantee that you would see a phenomenal business machine if everyone was so caring. The trade-off is that you have to let the employees taste what it's like to be business owners—to sense the control and the ability to change the business, to know the freedom of coming and going within the realm of propriety, to know the benefit of increased freedom commensurate to the effort that they put into it.

Some employees come to an organization and simply want to earn a check. They come and put in hours and expect a paycheck promptly at the end of that time period. What will it take to bring them out of that selfish cycle and into a realm of ownership? What would happen to them if they tasted the essence of ownership? They could change and begin bringing their ideas, their concerns and their hopes to the table. Some employees are out to move up the ladder of success irrespective of the feelings of others. What would happen to them if they were put in the place where they had to face those whom they have hurt; to walk through the process of forgiveness and the learning that comes from the hurts that they have caused in others? This process brings extreme freedom. How would that different type of freedom help them? What about the employee who takes ownership, who wants to be a leader and to invest his experience into his employer's organization, but who is held back because of a manager's fear? Perhaps the fear is that this employee will excel past him or that he will make a bad and costly decision? All these things can be handled on an exception-by-exception basis, and the outcome can be great, but it requires those in control to offer freedom to their employees—freedom to make decisions, freedom to take ownership, freedom to be wrong, freedom to take chances.

When I was just out of college, I began working for a consulting firm in the IT world. During the first week, most of my time was spent getting to know my boss and observing his work ethic. During that time, he had a conversation with me that will affect me for the rest of my life. He said, "Someday, you won't be working with me. It's inevitable that you will move on to other things in life. But, if I've done my job well, you'll never be satisfied working in Corporate America." When he told me this, I wondered what he meant. But, as the years sailed by I understood more fully the meaning of his words. When I began my job with him, my pay was 100 percent commission—I had no salary. He told me that I could take off as much time as I wanted and that I could work from home as often as I wanted as long as my responsibilities at the office were fulfilled and the meetings were attended. Over the nine years that I was employed by him, I watched how much he invested in me as his employee—how much trust, freedom and ownership he gave me. In return, I gave him hard and steady work, I was trustworthy, committed and I took ownership in his business. I treated every decision as though I were accountable to him for it. His investment in me yielded my investment back in him. When the nine years were over, he was right. There was no way I could ever be satisfied working for a controlling, demeaning and untrusting corporation. I had been permanently ruined. I had tasted freedom, and there was no way I could go back.

If you are in management, you may be reading this and thinking, "Sure, it sounds good, but in a business the size of ours, there's no way we could ever do this. It would be pandemonium." But you're wrong. You can and should give your employees the taste of freedom and the desire to own your business as much as you do—perhaps even more. If you start by honoring your employees with trust and allow them to flex their hours or take off an afternoon and make it up somewhere else in the week, or if you allow them to work from home every so often, the rewards will be immense. What you may be sensing but may be unwilling to put into words is that you will have to change—you will have to manage differently. To offer people freedom, you have to give up some control and start treating people as equals. But, as you do, I believe the experience of freedom is waiting for you as well.

As a manager of people, you know the stresses that are involved with doing your job. Wouldn't it be nice to have a group of people who are loyal to you beyond their duties? How about a group of people who would be willing to support you even if they don't agree with your decisions? What about being able to trust others to get your work done while you are gone from the office, or to free up your schedule so that you can begin offering your gifts and talents to your manager? If you are an owner and can go no higher, wouldn't you like to have people who you can trust to prosper and excel your business so that you can do other things that are important to you? You see, by promoting freedom in your staff, you end up reaping freedom as a manager, owner or primary controller in your business.

Please realize, I am not suggesting that you send out an e-mail to 25,000 employees and tell them, "Effective today, you may work flex hours and take lunches that are as long as you wish as long as you make up your hours later in the week." What I am saying is that as you look at your employees, begin calling them in and honoring them with freedom. One by one you will change the face and culture of your business. If it gets misused, challenge the person to a greater level of ownership. But don't give up on freedom—it is worth more than money and yields results in employees that are greater than any bonus check you may write.

Here are some thoughts on how to introduce the gift of freedom into your business culture:

1. Get past fear. You can't allow fear to guide your management of people. Even if you are afraid that people will take advantage of their newfound freedoms, you must press through and allow them to prove you wrong. The benefits reaped will far outweigh the costs of freedom; just don't give up.

2. Honor the individual. Each person may have a distinctively different idea of freedom. As you begin to invest in people and allow them to experience liberty, let the gift fit the person's lifestyle. In our busy world, spouses often work different shifts so that they seldom see each other. For that person, freedom might be to work from noon to nine instead of eight to five so that they have the morning with their spouse. To another person, it might simply be the flexibility to have freedom over their lunch schedule. Whatever you decide, talk with the person. Invite him or her to sit with you at your desk and say, "You are valuable to me. I see your work and the dedication you put into your job. Because you are such an asset, I want to honor you with some extra freedom. I know your spouse works from three to midnight every night, and so I want you to know that you have the freedom to shift your hours two days a week so that you can come in at noon and leave at nine. Would you like that? At least it will give you a couple of mornings with your spouse."

   Doing this will show your employee that you care about him. You have just honored him, you have just honored his spouse and more than likely, he will get a lot more work done in the evening hours when there are fewer disruptions. No matter what you may do, make it fit the individual and be certain that you express your appreciation to them and that your intent is to honor them for their dependability and service.

3. Don't issue a widespread "freedom" policy to every employee all at once. Freedom is something that is earned. Spend time talking with the employee about the type of freedom that you are giving. Explain that you are going to try it out for the next thirty days and then evaluate it during and after that time to

decide if that type of freedom is a good fit for the employee and for the business. If it is a good fit, then keep on going. If you do everything you can to help that employee flourish in that newfound freedom and yet they are unable to succeed, change it out for a more concrete freedom, such as shifting their workday by a half hour or offering them a flexible lunch schedule.

4. Don't be the bottleneck. Freedom is something that can only be administered as you change your management style as well. If you personally can't handle the huge change that giving freedom will bring to your work culture, then be certain to give it to one person at a time and allow yourself room to change in the process. What you will most likely find is that it's not the misconduct of your employees that is the hindrance to freedom, it is you. It means that you will have to be less controlling, you will have to work on better communication skills and you will have to trust people when you are not around to make certain that they are doing what you expect. But, if you are willing to change, I believe you will find that freedom will bring ownership, ownership will bring commitment and commitment will bring *you* freedom when all is said and done.

5. Deal with the exceptions on a case-by-case basis. Don't punish an entire body of workers for the misconduct of a few. As you are walking through this new field of experiences, give yourself the grace to learn and to see others misuse their freedom. Use the opportunities of misuse to instruct the employees and to invest in them. Abraham Lincoln said, "Nearly all men can stand adversity, but if you want to test a man's character, give him power." The same could be said of freedom. The true colors of any employee will come out when he realizes that the noose has been loosed. This new freedom will likely bring out pride and maybe even some cocky behavior. Don't be afraid to set the employee straight, but to also give him room to be wrong. He will need to learn how to set boundaries for himself, and as a coach and mentor, you can be there to help him

do it. Only as a last resort should you take away freedom, because once an employee has tasted it, he will do whatever he can to hold on to it.

6. People do what you inspect, not necessarily what you expect. If you choose to allow people the freedom to work from home, have them tell you what they intend to do while they are there. Also, have them give you an idea of how much time it will take to get it done. When they are finished, you'll need to check their work to see how much of it was completed. If they fail, be non-confrontational and ask them to be honest with you. Ask them to explain why they didn't get things done as they expected. Offer some possibilities like, "Did you find it difficult to focus?" or "Did you find that there were more interruptions than when you are here at the office?" Honor them by giving them the ability to troubleshoot the process with you.

   If they absolutely cannot think of reasons why they didn't accomplish the work goals that they had expected, then challenge them to keep a log of occurrences while working at home so that the next time you discuss it, they'll have a better idea of what's wrong. Have them record when they are interrupted and what the interruption is. If, after a second time, they can't complete their work and they still don't know why, simply explain to them that you want to find the solution together. Let them know that until they can help you make working at home more productive than working at the office, you'll have to hold off. Finally, encourage them to approach you any time they feel that they can offer a plan to make it more productive and you'll consider it.

7. Keep it simple. Checking for misuse of freedom doesn't have to be a difficult process full of forms and phone calls. In a personal circumstance, I had one of my employees e-mail me every couple of days with the work he was doing, and then I would see the work that he did as the completed product was turned in. By looking at the completed product and recalling what he said in the e-mails, I could tell if he was doing what

was expected of him. Because I was so familiar with the processes necessary to get the work done, I knew if a task should take an hour, two hours or more. If I saw that the work was taking more time than it should, I was able to correct him and keep him on track.

TWELVE

THE LEARNING CYCLE

It's amazing how some lessons in life just take longer than others to learn. Take my children, for example. Both of my kids are very bright. My son has the most amazing ability to make people laugh. My daughter is a loving and gentle soul. I know, it sounds like I'm bragging, but I would fail my job as a father if I didn't do so. The interesting thing about my kids is the amount of difference between them. They both have the same fabulous parents, they both come from the same loving home with the same rules and influences around them, and yet they learn things differently.

When my children were very young, I decided to teach them the difference between "yes" and "no." In my estimation of life, learning the difference between these two words is not only reasonable and necessary, but also the most difficult lesson to grasp. I'm amazed at the number of adults who have never mastered the understanding of these two terms. After all, how many times have you seen a marking that states "No U-turns" and then watched someone execute a speedy one just in front of the sign?

My young daughter took no time at all to figure out the difference between "yes" and "no." However, my son was a very different story. To teach this lesson to him, I sat him in front of me on my lap. I carried a shiny metallic pen and pencil set in my pocket, and my son loved to grab them. Because he loved them so much, I decided to capitalize on his urgency to grab them and use that experience to teach him "yes" and "no." You may think me a bit harsh to try and train my son this way, but I've never regretted it. Each time he would reach for the silver pen or pencil, I would say "no" and then plink his hand with my fingers just enough so that he would know there was consequence for his action. After three or four times, I figured he would understand that "no" meant "stop" or "don't" or "quit," but still, he proceeded on with great fervency. Pretty soon we were up to twenty times, his mind still set on seeing how far he could go and not get the plink on the hand. Each time he would reach for my pen, he would stare right into my eyes and trudge on ahead. In my mind, I was thinking, *Surely he'll get the idea*, but it wasn't long until we were at thirty tries. Finally, after forty tries, he put his hand ever so close to my pen, but then, after staring at my face, he would pull his hand away. With that, I would pat him on the back, give him hugs and tell him "yes" with great exuberance.

Once he figured out that a "yes" came with fanfare and that the consequences of the "yes" were much better than the consequences of the "no," keeping him from touching or even reaching for my pens was easy. For the past nine years, that lesson has stuck with him. When I say "stop" or "no" as his parent, his feet plant in the ground and he doesn't move. Spending that time with my boy produced three basic outcomes in his life. It taught him that dad didn't give up easily. It taught him that there were consequences when he heard "no" and continued on anyway. Finally, he learned that when I said "no," I meant "don't" and "stop" and "quit." That experience would set the stage for a great number of other lessons he would learn over the next nine years. He had just gone through The Learning Cycle.

It was earlier in life when I first became familiar with this cycle. I graduated from high school with a very low GPA. This is embarrassing, but if memory serves me correctly, I was 93rd in my class. My whole class of 235 students must have been hundredths of a points away from one another because my GPA was 2.3. I didn't enjoy high school, and I just wanted to get through it. But, by the time I got to college, I had determined to make something of myself and was interested in what I was learning.

Each new semester and each new class I would start, I would remind myself that the first two weeks were a part of The Learning Cycle. I would observe my instructor, watching his gestures, how he taught, how he addressed the class and what seemed important to him. I watched for cues like, "I like..." and "This is important..." Out of those I would create a mental profile of who he was. Inevitably, I would go to him and have a one-on-one conversation where I would find out about his policies on classwork and extra-credit and, finally, the most valuable question of all: "What do you feel is the most important thing I should know about homework and your class?" I would make a point to sit front and center in every class so that I could express to the instructor that he was important and what he had to say was interesting.

That first two weeks would set the course for the rest of the semester. I had not only become a student of the subject but a student of my instructor as well. Because I spent so much time identifying the things that

> **The Learning Cycle is the quintessential process by which the rest of any given experience takes its direction.**

were important to my professors, I was able to mold my classwork around their individual personalities as well as their likes and dislikes. Because of this, and because of some hard work, I graduated with a 4.0 GPA. I firmly believe this all happened because I took time to work hard and to walk through The Learning Cycle.

The Learning Cycle is the quintessential process by which the rest of any given experience takes its direction. Whether you are sitting in a classroom observing a new teacher or in front of a prospective client, at lunch with a new volunteer or at a meeting table with a board of directors, it's important to become a student of this new prospect that has entered your life. You need to learn what this prospect wants, what they need and what they expect to accomplish. You need to do this so that you can effectively meet your personal goals and lead them into the realization that you are meeting theirs, too. You may have heard some people say, "Know your audience." But The Learning Cycle is much deeper than this. It goes beyond learning what is necessary to convince someone you are right or to purchase your goods and services.

After you've walked through this process, you will understand better why people act the way they do. You will understand their needs and wants and then be able to fairly assess your strengths and talents to see if you can help those people reach their goals. The goal is to become so familiar with your prospects that you not only know what they want but are able to provide it when they want it and with a minimal amount of instruction.

I believe this is an item that is learned rather than earned. You can't earn the right to know what someone else needs and to what degree it is important to them. You can only learn that by observation, by caring enough to watch the finest points of his or her personality and then trying to invest yourself into his or her life's goals.

When you start The Learning Cycle, you make a willful decision to lay down what you feel about a person, group or entity and to let your observations and your desire to learn the truth about them guide you to the next step of your relationship. You choose to blend your talents with their needs and to design a solution that fits them and that is rewarding to you. You choose to put them in front of yourself and to make them the more important thing; to place them above yourself and your own will.

As you walk through The Learning Cycle, here are some things to keep in mind:

1. Be selfless. Don't focus only on what you want to know about someone; focus on what they want you to know about themselves, which may be two entirely different things. Keep in mind that you are trying to learn so that you can bypass your

differences and help them accomplish their goals, while at the same time, seeing benefit for yourself. But, be careful not to get those two turned around. It has to be "they" first and "me" second.

2. Be sensitive. Don't be forceful. Don't push people to open up to you. Don't push people to tell you what you want to know. Let people tell you about themselves as they see fit and as they feel the freedom to do it. It may be that as you try to learn about someone's personality and wants, that because of hurts or difficulties in his life, that person simply won't let you into his world or even elaborate about it to the slightest degree. If this is the case, just do your best and hope for an opportunity to get to know him better at a later time. But don't push. Just go on. If you have difficulty getting someone to express himself to you—to let you know what he expects or hopes for, familiarize yourself with the chapter entitled "Everyone Loves to Teach" This may be of help to you.

3. Be teachable. If you are unwilling to learn how others process life and about what is important to them, you may as well never start this process. This experience is reserved for those who can trade their own selfishness for the anticipation that by learning about someone else, they will become more useful, helping others to advance in their goals. This is not for self-seekers. If you want to do things your own way and you intend to go into this process to convince others that they are wrong and you are right, you may as well stop now. No mere mortal has the power to change anyone, only to influence someone...for good or for bad. Choose to use your influence to learn from the knowledge and experience of others, and then use that newfound knowledge to help them reach their goals. By doing this, you will become more knowledgeable, and you will be better able to meet your own needs.

4. Give them what they want. Once you've gone through all these steps, pump out what your prospect expects to see, whether it's work done a certain way, sales happening in certain months,

or effort directed during specific seasons of the year. Whatever their motivating passion, help them achieve it with your self-less work. Take your talents and invest them in their goals. By doing this, you will see your own goals fulfilled.

THIRTEEN

HOW TO BE GREAT IN YOUR JOB

There are many ways to get ahead in this world, and each of them has their own catalyst. You can learn to play the political game by bending the truth, portraying things in shades of gray and building allegiances that you hope will weld your place in the corporate structure. You can brownnose and suck your way up the corporate ladder. You can play dirty pool and destroy the character of people around you so that no one is left to defend the lair but you. You can pretend to be nice to everyone and then use your sharp tongue to impale the backs of anyone that gets in your way. Unfortunately, these are all common practices in the world as we know it today.

However, none of these strategies yield such solid results as simply and faithfully serving. If you consider everyone as better than you and your goal is to make them look good, you win any way you go. If you are serving your superiors, your management appreciates you because you are willing to do the work without taking the credit. If you are serving your coworkers, should any of your peers be in line for a promotion, you will probably be remembered for your servant heart. If it's your direct reports, they will only esteem you for your willingness to get in the trenches and consider them your peers.

How often have you been in a situation where you have done work or made suggestions that your manager has taken ownership of? More than likely, your first response was to be frustrated that you didn't get the credit. But, if you continue past this point and let him take credit for the positive change, you will endear yourself to many a manager, and he'll have you helping him on future projects.

While working for a client of mine, I was asked to go with him to a large meeting at the state level. The conversation was to determine the status of $25 million in funding that the client was hoping to receive. There was a lot riding on this meeting, and due to the tenor of the meeting and because the client didn't know what to expect, the then-reigning president asked that I go with them to the capitol.

When we arrived at the meeting, we were greeted by a number of high officials from the state, and we were asked to be seated. Little by little, the questions were asked, and when the president of my corporate client needed answers that I could give, he would lean over to me and make his request. Since I had written the system that was used to track all the data, I was keenly aware of how to pull it together into a usable format with little effort. Piece by piece, I would give him the resulting statistics and numbers. Finally, at the end of the meeting, the state officials requested subsets of data from my system. They asked if we could deliver it to them in two to three weeks. Within three minutes, I had pulled this data together. I gave it to the president, who then handed it to the state officials as he shook hands with them before leaving. Later, when we received feedback from the state about the meeting, they were amazed at the speed in which the president was able to deliver their requests. Ultimately, the contract was awarded, and the $25 million in revenues was theirs.

Certainly, I don't pretend to tell you that they received the contract solely due to my giving the requested answers to the president, but I am suggesting that it played a part in their decision. When they looked at the president of that corporation, they saw a man who was able to get what he wanted when he wanted it and with little effort. They saw that he could deliver to them what they wanted in short order. In their eyes, he looked good. All that I, and those on the contract team, did was to serve the president of that corporation. The state didn't look at any of us and proclaim our names off of the top of the capitol building. Nor did they come to me and shake my hand for being such a wonderful asset to the president of that corporation. I and the others simply made it our jobs to make him look as good as we could and to give him what he needed as often as possible.

What would have happened if I, or anyone else that was on that contract team, had tried to steal the attention in a selfish attempt to prove our worth to the authorities from the state? It would have conveyed that the organization was unruly, unkempt and unable to work together under the leadership of one man. It would have conveyed the president of the corporation was no true leader at all. It would have forced the state to consider how much they really wanted to risk by placing their trust in such an unpolished head.

When we are selfless about who gets the credit for something, we get the joy of relaxing in our work and believing that those who need to will ultimately reward us for our labors. This goes against everything inside of us because it is like dying each time you give your talent and knowledge for someone else's reputation. But, Jesus informed us of a wonderful law, which states that whatever you give away will be given back to you in a greater amount. If you show people that you are interested in helping them succeed then you can expect faithful, honest people to work alongside of you because they will know you are trustworthy and honest. If you invest in others and make them look good, you can expect to be invested in and made to look good, too.

As you practice serving, remember the following:

1. You must be selfless. Always make others look better than yourself. You can't give freely if you are always concerned about getting or becoming.

2. You must guard your heart. Oftentimes, people don't know how to receive this type of labor. They feel you are brown-

nosing or have some kind of agenda. If you truly serve and it is repaid with criticism and mistrust, let it roll off your back. Only time and persistence can change this type of response. During this time, don't be offended, and don't be discouraged. Just keep trying.

3. You must be patient. If this is new to you, your biggest enemy will be you. You'll be angry with yourself for letting opportunities get away. You'll be frustrated with yourself for not fighting more. Just remember, you're changing the way you see things. What you call an opportunity now may have a different face in six months. Be willing to give yourself room to grow and change. You may need it.

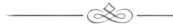

FOURTEEN

THIS IS SELF-CORRECTING

With so many battles raging around us, it's important to realize our limitations. We deal with other's emotions and our emotions; we deal with coworkers' inadequacies and our own inadequacies; we deal with abused authority and our own frustrations with abused authority. There are so many opportunities to become frustrated, disheartened, exasperated, angry and dejected that we really don't need to go looking for things to add to our emotional and professional plates. These things tend to lock on to us like heat-seeking missiles and cause our thoughts to be as discombobulated as a handful of bobby pins inside an MRI unit.

Because these stressors are so prevalent, we can't carry all of them or we'll break. There is not a man or woman on the surface of the earth that has been created to haul an extreme load for any length of time—whether it be physical, emotional or professional.

> **With great power comes great responsibility.**

So, how do you keep the stressors down to a minimum, increase your productivity and keep yourself out of trouble with your boss all at the same time? Evaluate the situation and ask yourself this question, "Is this self-correcting?" If the answer is "yes," then you have discovered one more key to unlocking yourself from a heavy burden.

With great power comes great responsibility, and this is a powerful rule. Without care, you could go too far to the left or too far to the right. To use this rule effectively requires careful practice. But, once you master its use, you will be amazed at how freeing it is to reduce your life's issues by one more battle that would have stolen your time, emotion and resources.

The imaginations we create are generally perfect, ignoring or muting out anything that could foil our expectations. Many times a week, you deal with people who have used their imagination to define truth instead of searching diligently for it. As an example, let me sketch a mental picture. Your manager comes to you and informs you that he expects everyone using staples to account for the number of staples they consume on a daily basis. He needs to know how many were used, and for which client, so that the staples can be billed out as a production expense. Having worked as line staff and with quite a bit of recent experience in the field, you perceive that there could be a hesitancy with your coworkers when they realize they must fill out an online staple tracking sheet at the bottom of each hour. You tell your boss that you feel the employees may be a little sensitive about this and may not buy in to the process. You tell him it's just a hunch, but that you are pretty certain they won't fill out the online form accurately or consistently. Then, from behind a Cheshire cat smile, he replies, "Thank you for your opinion. It matters a lot. Now, I gave you a mandate; it's your responsibility to carry it out." What do you do? You figure out the straightest path between two points and walk it. Then, go on with life and let it go. It's self-correcting.

You may think this a humorous anecdote, but the truth couldn't be closer to your grasp. How many times have you run across experiences that were so extremely frustrating that you wanted to retaliate but felt the prison term wasn't worth the effort? You can see the problem, you can see that the proposed solution won't work, and yet, no one will listen to you. Then, to add insult to injury, the problems that will arise by following this so-called solution directly affect your area of concern. That means you will be the one having to clean up the mess in the end. As frustrating as this may be, you must realize that no matter how hard you try to fight the process, you are destined to lose because the political waters you are skiing in are shark-infested, and the only people who have the shark repellant are too busy steering the boat into the most beautiful sunset they have ever imagined. So, now you are faced with a dilemma. You ask yourself, "Do I continue to fight and possibly sacrifice my position and future with my employer? Or, do I calmly vocalize my concerns, go along for the ride (knowing that it's going to be inconvenient) and just do as I'm told, hoping that sooner or later management will see that this solution is as futile as I had suggested?" To answer this question, first ask yourself, "Is this self-correcting?" If it is self-correcting, you're done. Consider it job security. Not only will you and your coworkers get to enact the process, you'll get to clean up after it's done.

In the real world, a client of mine had some simple paperwork that needed to be carefully filled out and then submitted for payment. I and other key people worked with the line staff, trained them and then asked them to complete the paperwork properly, but they ignored our requests. So, we went to the manager of the division and explained the necessity of putting a corrective action plan in place since this was affecting over $20,000 per month in revenue. But, try as we might, we could not get him to move on our behalf. Finally, after a short meeting, the key staff and I decided to let it run its course. We knew that we would have a huge mess to clean up when we were done, but we realized that our political losses would far outweigh any gains we might realize. As time went on, the amount of loss had mushroomed into something that became interesting to the manager we had approached just a few months earlier. Suddenly, our request made sense and carried a weight all its own. Despite everything we had tried before, we had made no progress at any level. But, when the pain grew intense enough, all of a sudden, our request carried value because it was the only piece of the puzzle that was missing. That was a self-correcting situation.

If you've never looked at situations in this light before, you'll find that you probably take on quite a few self-correcting situations that, had you let them run their natural course, would have left you with more energy, more joy and less stress in your life. I'm amazed at how many battles I have not had to fight because, after evaluating them, I concluded that they were self-correcting. I would state my concerns, state the reason for my position and then just do what was requested of me. The benefits far outweighed the costs because after experiencing a handful of these situations, my opinions mattered much more and my value to the organization escalated.

Of course, there are those times when you think you know what you're doing, and you are the one who is wrong. Certainly, there have been times when I was the bad decision maker. But, since my understanding was flawed, and I didn't know it was flawed, I still went through the same steps and started by vocalizing my concerns. After not seeing any fruit from my input and concluding that it was self-correcting, I chose to be silent and not to argue the point. Amazingly, because I chose to let the problem correct itself and not to force an argument, the solution I thought was flawed actually worked and I gained value as a team player and as someone who wasn't always set on getting his own way.

When deciding whether or not a situation is self-correcting, keep the following in mind:

1. Be responsible. Don't use this skill to convince yourself that it's all right to let others do your job and to complete your responsibilities. There is no excuse for laziness or low personal expectations.

2. Be caring. If you are the president of a huge corporation or if you are sacking groceries at your local supermarket, you have to care about what happens to the people around you. Using this rule for selfish personal or political gain is very uncaring and wrong. Don't ever get to the point where you say, "Hey, serves him right. He can fall on his face. After all, it's self-correcting." If you ever catch yourself saying or thinking this, then it's not self-correcting. You are actually expecting failure, and that is not good for you, your coworkers, your employer or your own business.

3. Be a listener. You never know when someone will have a better idea than you do, so sit back and listen to what everyone
else has to say. If they are wrong, you'll allow them to exhaust
themselves on each other so that by the time you present your
concerns, most other opinions have already been stated and
you'll be recognized for bringing fresh meat to the table.

4. Be unafraid. When it is appropriate, you must present your concerns. After all, you are part of the team. Don't use the phrase,
"it's self-correcting" as a way of consoling yourself because you
are shy or you don't want to take the chance of being wrong. If
you are fearful for any reason, if you are legitimately concerned
that the decision is incorrect or if you have some kind of input
that could benefit the process, break past your fears and lay your
cards on the table. Even if you are chuckled at or even pounced
upon after doing it, don't let it wound your spirit. I've been
amazed at the times where such an occurrence has happened and
where that input was actually used in the final resolution of the
issue. You never know if what you have to offer will be part of
the solution until it's brought into the open and challenged. And
if it isn't used, then at least you helped narrow down the resolution by the process of elimination. I have told numerous clients,
"You don't know what you want until you realize what you don't
want." So, even if all you do is help the organization realize what
they don't want, relax in the fact that it still carries weight.

5. Go easy on yourself. When you choose to let go of a sensitive
situation—to let it take its course because you have more to
lose than to gain by continuing to fight—go easy on yourself,
your coworkers, your managers and the decision-makers because there will be an adjustment period for everyone involved.
Each person will need to have some adjusting room. Realize,
too, that your level of frustration will be proportionate to your
level of competitiveness until you learn to absolutely let go
while these situations correct themselves.

6. Don't sabotage. Don't walk through the situation constantly
trying to prove that you are right and others are wrong. When

the decision is made, try with all your might to make it work, and if it fails, you will have no regrets. Equally as important, you have proven yourself to be a team player who is not a spoiled child and who can continue to bring great value to an organization even when you don't get your way.

FIFTEEN

YOU ARE NOT RESPONSIBLE FOR WHAT YOU SAY

To help you grasp this truth, I will offer an example that spans both genders. Ladies, you are first. Just imagine. It's the eve of the New Year. Tonight, you have the most romantic, most spectacular night of your life planned. You have decided to surprise the most important man in your life with an amazing array of experiences that will take you well into New Year's Day. To build the anticipation, you have dropped hints about this evening for the past couple of weeks— nothing that anyone could piece together, but hints that will make sense when they come together on your special evening.

Since your date is an avid fan of dragsters, you decide to treat him to an eye-candy experience of a pre-dinner car expo. As you walk in the door of the expo centre, your senses are immediately bombarded with a triad of sound, sight and smell. You hear the engines revving; you smell the odor of nitrous and as you begin to walk around the show floor, you decide you're going to venture out of your safety zone a little and try to make a comment or two that will show the man you love that you want to be involved in his life—even in play time. You wait until you find what you consider to be the most impressive vehicle with the widest array of gauges and gadgets and the most detailed paint job. As you approach the car, the fact that your hearing begins to fail is an obvious sign that the engine is running. To be heard by your evening's companion, you know that you must yell above the noise. Simultaneously, the engine is cut as you shout at the top of your lungs, "This guy is beautiful! What detail!" So proud you are of your attempt to fit in that you don't realize everyone in the room is now staring at you and your date. Then, a voiceless, "Thank you," is heard from the aftermath of the vehicle's roar. From beside the car walks its owner: a 6' 4" physically perfect specimen with the classic Roman jaw line, cut physique and model appearance. You hadn't noticed him before because you were so intent on trying to involve yourself in the likes and interests of your date. At that moment, the man who has you on his arm stares at you for a couple of moments with a scowl on his face. You stare back but simply don't understand what's going on. You decide to let it pass and to enjoy the rest of the show. After an hour of frustrated, one-word conversations, you decide that it's finally time to eat. Grateful to get out of the exhaust fumes for fear that your date is being badly effected by them, you gleefully grab his hand and lead him to your vintage '68 Bug and take him to the most romantic seafood restaurant in town.

You walk into this beautiful restaurant arm in arm. He is finally warming up again, and when he looks at you, there is something about his stare that bespeaks anticipation of what will happen next. As you follow the maître d' to your specially reserved table, your date perks up. As he strolls down the corridor with you, he murmurs to himself just loud enough for you to hear, "Look at those legs. Oh man!" You look ahead of you and, about twenty feet away, you see a beautiful, dark-haired, long-legged, Italian fashion model. You become incensed that he would stoop to such horrible expressions of his manhood—that he would say such things in front of you, much less say such things at all. Immediately, you become hurt and angered that he would have eyes for another woman so you shut down.

You sit silently at the table for the next twenty-five minutes through your appetizer and your salad. During this time, he is trying to figure out why you are so upset with him, while simultaneously working to forgive you for belittling and embarrassing him so badly at the car show. You begin to wonder what you ever saw in this man who would betray your good spirit and loving intent by daring to cast a glance upon another woman. Finally, he decides to try and bridge the cavernous rift that is separating you, even though you are sitting at the same table. "Why are you upset? What'd I do?" With that, you unload your frustration about "the other woman." When he hears your bitter diatribe, he immediately becomes defensive. What you had not observed was that as your guest came through the entrance and walked down the corridor with you on his right arm, there on his left was a tank holding the most beautiful and gigantic crabs that he had ever seen. An avid lover of shellfish, his interest was piqued, and in that split second, he had expressed to himself what he would be ordering for dinner. But by this time, you were already frustrated beyond apology, which only infuriated him more. "Besides, isn't this the pot calling the kettle black?" He starts his counterattack and volleys his frustration back at you regarding the hunk of beef you so openly yelled about at the car show. You try to explain that you were only attempting to make conversation and to support him; that you weren't talking about the man, you were talking about the car. But, by this time he, too, is beyond frustration. When all is said and done, you both decide that the only way out of this death trap—the only way to preserve your relationship—is to trust each other one more time and let it go. Later in the evening, as you think back, you even laugh at the misunderstanding. But, what did you learn from all of this? You learned that you are not responsible for what you say, you're responsible for what people hear.

One interesting thing about communication is that it takes shape only after it has passed from our lips or fingers through an invisible, yet powerful dust cloud made up of the experiences, frustrations, hurts, culture, conviction, need and greed of the recipient. This cloud can strip meaning and it can add to it. Consider how weight is added to our words. As words leave us and pass through our recipient's dust cloud, aspects of what we say attract particles from the cloud, just like a magnet attracts iron shavings. As our words pass through, a piece of hurt affixes itself to what we have said. Continuing through the cloud, pieces of prejudice fly through the air and plink themselves onto the sides of what we've said. By the time our words get through the cloud, they are much heavier because they are carrying a lot more weight than when they began. They land in the soul, where the intellect of the recipient begins to process them and, finally, they are felt by the emotions.

Conversely, it is also possible for that powerful, invisible dust cloud to strip away the weight of what we say, much like a sand blaster can strip away layer after layer of wood. By the time our words pass through the cloud and are diminished by the swiftly swirling particles of fear, anger, hurt and skepticism, they may have no weight at all. Simple sentences such as, "That's interesting," "You look nice today," "I've never tasted something like this before," "I love you" and "Thank you" can get skewed way out of context. There's nothing special about these phrases by themselves. It's the extra weight that is either added to or stripped away from them as they pass through this cloud that makes them impotent or lethal.

I remember a medical facility that I had taken on as a client a few years back. I had agreed to construct a software package to track all of their Medicaid reimbursements throughout the year. The data they were keying into the system was horribly flawed. I asked, "Who is responsible for this data? This is pretty messed up." While I should have been more careful about what I was saying, I was just making a simple statement of truth. It wasn't intended to be a tirade against any specific person. But, that isn't the way my comment was interpreted. I was immediately corrected for being mean and accusatory. All I was trying to say was, "Who has access to this data? We need to share some training tips on how to keep it cleaner than it is. It's not irreparable; it just needs some love and attention." Had I said what I meant rather than assuming that the other person would trust that I was on his side and not against him, then I could have diffused the situation from the beginning. Since, at that moment, I hadn't realized the value of what you are now reading, I put myself in situation after situation that could have been avoided, all because I didn't care enough about what others heard instead of what I said.

Another circumstance took place while helping a not-for-profit organization work through a capital campaign for a new building they wanted to construct. Part of the capital campaign included creating a way for donors to bring their stocks to the NFP so that they could get the donation pre-tax and at the original cost of the donor's stock transaction. If the giver would make their donation before converting it to cash, they only had to claim the original cost of the stocks as the donation value and not the value of the stocks at the time of donation. If the stocks increased in value, this would mean fewer taxes to be paid on the donated value. To accomplish this, we needed a clearing account into which we could transfer these donated stocks. A friend of mine was a series seven broker (different from the one you may have already read about) and could help us with our needs. However, he was an employee of an organization and didn't have the final say on the agreed-upon rates of transfer and fees for service. So, at the end of our meeting, I asked my friend to fax us a document that outlined the transfer costs and account fees so that we would have something in writing for our records. When I did this, his appearance immediately changed, and he became very cold and defensive.

What I found out a number of days later through a mutual friend was that he had been offended by my conversation. Although he would never confess it to me, and although every attempt that I made to rectify the situation failed, it was obvious that there was a huge change in the way he approached me that lasted for months. Looking back, I should have seen that he would have perceived my request as an attack of distrust, but the request and paperwork was necessary for proper business practice and to prove later that we were showing no favoritism based on our relationship. What should I have done? I should have been more concerned with how he heard my words rather than what I needed to say to fulfill my job requirements.

Given that you can't change the receiver of your words, what elements can you change to increase the chance that the recipient will hear and perceive what you are really trying to communicate? Here are some ideas:

1. Tell people why. Add words like "because" and "for" to your vocabulary, and use them even when you think they are unnecessary. When you take the time to express *why* something is the way it is, not only do you honor the recipient of your words, but you also help alleviate even more misunderstandings that could happen in the future. If you just had a fight with your spouse, a friend or a coworker and you attempt to straighten things out, saying "I'm sorry" has weight and usually makes it through the dust cloud at least 50 percent intact. But sending the word package, "I'm sorry because I was wrong. I was selfish and should have listened instead of speaking" through the cloud will yield a much finer reward because there's not much that can be misunderstood or misread.

2. Give advanced warning. Tell your receiver what you are going to talk about before you start. For example, you might tell him that you want to talk about something that is very sensitive and could be misunderstood and then encourage him to ask as many questions as he needs to in an attempt to make certain that he understands. Giving people warning on sensitive issues is almost always better than just springing it on them.

   In my stock donation example above, I should have opened the conversation with the following declarative, "Thanks for coming. Before we get started, I want to be certain that you understand that we will be talking about transfers and services and that we are asking all prospective agents to furnish us with a reply in writing, outlining the terms and costs agreed upon during our conversation. This is just standard and we are requesting it from everyone. Will that be okay with you?" Doing this would have diffused the situation by keeping him in the know and removing the appearance that we were just having him follow this procedure because he couldn't be trusted. It also would have given him the chance to express himself because I would have ended with a request for his permission to continue on.

3. Tell people their value. Before saying something that may hurt your listener, reaffirm his worth. If you have to deliver difficult information that could be seen as an attack against the receiver's character or worth, first let him know how strongly you care about him, and be specific about why. But don't just stop there. Get him to verbally affirm that he understands and believes that you care for him and that you would never hurt or purposely attack him. Only after you have offered your support and gotten his approving response to your offering of faith, love and goodness should you begin to approach the more sensitive issue at hand.

4. Use the phrase, "Okay, I'm done." If you are nervous about what you need to say, ask your receiver to listen without interrupting. Tell him that when you are done, you will say, "Okay. I'm done." Let him know that when he hears those words— only then are you open for questions. Help him realize that what you are going to say is very difficult. You must have his complete attention or it will not be possible for him to fully understand what you are trying to communicate.

5. Listen with fresh ears. Ask someone to repeat back to you what he understood you to say. When you get done talking about your subject, simply say, "Now, tell me what you think I said." Then listen carefully and try not to assign the same value to his words as you have assigned to your own. Listen not so much to what he is saying but to what he is not saying. Is he lacking any details that you already said? Is he missing any important

details that you simply forgot to say? Listening with fresh ears will help you find those potholes and fill them in.

6. Practice. If you have to deal with something that is very difficult, be certain to think through what you are going to say before speaking a word. Your imagination is skilled at carrying on two-sided conversations. How many times have you been angry at someone else and carried on a conversation in your mind that was made up of what you were going to say and what they were going to say? Then you decided what you would reply and what they would reply. And before you realized it, twenty minutes had gone by—all wasted on your imaginary argument. Harness that powerful capability for your benefit rather than for your destruction. As you imagine your conversation, put yourself in the other person's place and imagine how he will feel when you are done. Then, go back and fill in the blanks. Keep doing this until you are secure that you have developed as much definition as possible. If necessary, use notes. In sensitive situations, you should never consider this cheating.

7. Don't use e-mail. Never use e-mail to discuss or represent any issue that could even be slightly construed as confrontational or divisive. Always carry out sensitive conversations in person. Be certain to read the next chapter, Hiding Behind E-mail, for a more thorough discussion on this topic.

SIXTEEN

HIDING BEHIND E-MAIL

After working for your employer these past seven years, you get to enjoy two weeks of vacation…all at once! But now that relaxing break is over, and it's time to go back to work. You know that there will be some catch-up to do, but that's okay. You're a hard worker. You put in hour after hour to get things done and to get them done right. You don't like sloppy work, and you don't like to clean up sloppy messes that could have been avoided by the simple application of some common sense. Your frustration rises as you look on your desk and see a stack of requests that have been placed in your basket. These are not normal requests, however. These are improperly completed requests. Your blood begins to simmer as you start to wade through the stack of forms, realizing all the work you will now have to do to clean up this trash pit of paper that someone else has so generously bestowed upon you. By the time you get down to page 128 in your stack of forms, you are now boiling. Not only do you have to track down nine different managers to get their signatures, you have to fill in the extension column on every row and total it down for a grand total on each page so that they can be keyed into the accounting system and expense checks can be cut.

Upon further investigation of these beleaguered little forms, and after making a handful of calls to the fillers out of said forms, you realize that they all came from the same division, nay from the same department, and all have the same manager: Bob. A flurry of memories and past experiences engulfs your mind like a blizzard. Even though you haven't had problems in the past month or so, it's all just too real to forget. You've dealt with Bob before. Bob is what you would call, in laymen's terms, inept. More than once you have talked with Bob about the responsibilities of his employees and the proper way to fill out forms and requests. You've even babysat him when it was convenient. But, this is absolutely the last straw. No longer will you cower to the idol of customer service if it means enabling a ham-fisted incompetent to continue getting away with this kind of gross negligence.

You grab your phone in one hand, and with the other you take your mouse and stumble through your contact list to get his number. As you double click on his contact entry, your brain sparks and you are fully ignited. You put the phone down and you pen a scathing e-mail to Bob explaining how tired you are of him pulling this kind of farce and how his negligence is causing you more work. With a grimace that turns into a gleeful smile, you stare approvingly at your finished product, and you click the send button.

Your conscience now soothed, you jump back into the valuable work that you provide in exchange for your meager paycheck—that work, right now, is finishing all of Bob's work. You pat your conscience on the back for watching over the prosperity of your employer and for helping to correct such a waste of resources. A few moments later, your e-mail alert sounds. Already, you have received a reply from Bob. You're ready for a fight but discover that it's an out of office reply. Apparently, Bob's mother was vacationing in England and was killed in a tragic accident Wednesday before last—just two days after you went on vacation. He, like you, chose to take some time off of work; time to deal with his own loss as well as the liquidation of his mother's estate as its executor. The reply also states that your e-mail will be forwarded to Janice, Bob's manager, so that it can be handled promptly.

With the speed of summer lightning, you go to your sent folder, click on the e-mail you slashed out and request its recall, but it's too late. Soon your e-mail alert sounds again. This time it's an out of office reply from Janice. The memorial service for Bob's mother was today and evidently, she went to be a support for him. Immediately, you try to think of every faithful allegiance, every personal debt and any blackmail material you have on the IT department. You ask yourself, "Who can I call for the personal favor of deleting that e-mail before it's too late?" "Ding!" You look and there is a third e-mail. "Please come to my office." It's signed by Garry, the VP of finance.

As you are cleaning out your desk, you can't believe that you could have handled

> **In a fit of emotion, you reacted in writing.**

the situation so poorly. In a fit of emotion, you reacted in writing because you didn't want to deal with Bob face-to-face. If you would have just gone to Bob or called him on the phone like you had first planned to do, none of this would have happened. Had you chosen that route, you would have discovered that since Bob was absent, his secretary was simply distributing everything she could in an attempt to keep Bob's workload down so that he wouldn't have to face the added stress after returning from the loss of his mother. There is a positive side, though. As you are doing your new job in the mail room, you will have an abundance of hours to think about how you can handle this type of situation better the next time around.

The long-term effects of a situation like the one described here are many. You have to deal with the aftermath of the VP's frustration at your insensitivity. You have to face Bob, knowing you were wrong. And, you will have to deal with the reputation that you have formed by handling this situation the way you did. This reputation may not be resurrected for months, or possibly years.

The main reason that people use e-mail for sensitive issues is out of fear. Fear causes us to do any number of things. Generally speaking, until we learn to properly deal with fear, we can never go forward. Every one of us deals with the fear of rejection, the fear of revenge and the fear of rebuttal when we are confronted with a serious and sensitive issue. Precious few of us want to be hurt or to deal with the aftermath of such experiences. Amazingly, the techniques that we use to avoid fear often only feed the monster rather than slaying it. Techniques like ignoring the problem, talking to others about it in a derogatory manner and even laughing about it are all ways to feed the beast rather than banishing it, and leading the avoidance pack is e-mail. It can be the most passive-aggressive tool in any person's arsenal. What other tool can you use to get instant relief and gratification from your frustration, find license to be venomous (even in a politically correct way), retaliate completely with a full insurgent attack and remain completely untouched by the faceless recipient of your vengeance? It is inevitable, however, that the matter will only worsen if you don't attack it face-on, and ultimately it will grow stronger and attack you.

While conflict is certainly not pleasant, you have to build up your resistance to it so that you aren't afraid of it. Humble yourself. Assume that you can be wrong. Try to remember, "It's never you and me, it's always us and we." And then, gently walk through those trying situations, face-to-face, because an e-mail is not the answer. In the faceless, one-sided e-mail, there is no way to hear someone's hurt; there is no way to see the pain in someone's eyes; there is no way to ask questions; there is no way to know that someone understands you; there is no way to express that you are joking; there is no way to express your fear. These subsets of communication can and must only happen in a face-to-face conversation—even if it is a highly emotional and sensitive one—especially if it is a highly emotional and sensitive one.

Here then are some suggestions on when to use e-mail:

1. Stick to generics. Written communication types such as e-mail should be reserved for communicating general, non-emotional facts; recording historical, financial and legal valuables; explaining policy in a general, cross-platform sense; expressing general rules and regulations; and conveying dates, times and financial information.

2. Beware of emotion. If you are determined to write a document, and you sense even the slightest amount of emotion, stop right where you are and quit writing. Instead, spend your time making a list of items to cover, schedule a meeting with whoever needs to be involved and then speak of it in person. Never argue using e-mail.

3. Beware of assumptions. Written documents should always deal with hard facts, never assumptions, unless they are specifically notated in the document as such. In a face-to-face conversation, your assumptions can be challenged before being accepted as fact. This is not possible in a written form of communication. Be certain that you always notate your assumptions or you may suffer great embarrassment should you publish them as fact and then be proven wrong. As in the story above, there is oftentimes no way of recalling the information once it has been sent.

4. Beware of personals. Don't use e-mail for anything personal that you don't want seen by someone else. If you are dealing with sensitive issues in your life or someone else's, keep those conversations to in-person and phone conversations. Your e-mail wouldn't be the first to be blind carbon-copied to any number of other people, or possibly posted on a web board somewhere on the farthest outposts of the Internet.

5. Beware of gossip. Even if you're upset with someone, don't use e-mail for disseminating slanderous or defamatory information about other people. I guarantee you, within moments, the person who is the subject of the e-mail will get a copy from a loyal friend, and life as you know it will cease to exist. If you receive this type of e-mail, as soon as you see that it's gossip, delete it. Whatever you do, never reply or forward it—even if you feel like it's a chance to get even.

SEVENTEEN

WHEN PARTING IS NOT SUCH SWEET SORROW

My client was examining a contract that was gigantic to them. Were they to successfully complete the bid process and be chosen as a health services provider, the new workload would double their corporate size in a matter of three months. The bid process was tedious, taking over eight months from start to finish. When all bids were evaluated, they were selected to do the work. They were notified of their award in the beginning of March, and they had to be up and running on July 1 of the same year.

We began the arduous process of looking for software to manage their new business. We had presenters and sales people from a handful of professional software companies show us their wares. In the end, I was forced to deliver a scary report—a report I had hoped would not need to be delivered. I explained that they could use "Company A," who would charge them exorbitantly for support; they could use "Company B," who was one of their competitors and from whom they had just taken the contract; or I could develop a system from scratch and allow them to use it. Desiring ongoing freedom from service fees and not wanting their heads to be stuck in the guillotine of enemy control, they decided to use a system that I would develop specifically around the new contract guidelines that they had just received.

"Can you do it?" I was asked. "You only have two-and-a-half months to get it up and running." After some soul searching, as well as a good long conversation with my wife, I decided to take on the task. I would focus from sunrise to far past sundown on the data, the laws, the federal governmental guidelines and requirements, the expectations of HIPAA, the expectations for Medicaid and the list went on. To do so, I had to find a place where my wife would have extra support while I was working an inordinate number of hours and where I could do it without too much guilt. The obvious answer was my in-laws. I buried myself in a little town of about twelve hundred people and found the most exanimate place that I could to do my research—the public library.

After getting the system in my head, I began writing the code. For twelve or more hours a day, I poured myself into the creation of that system until I was unable to think. After I had spent so much time memorizing the contract, as well as the federal and state guidelines, I became the go-to for contract questions and clarifications. I began working with two other ladies to create the standard operating procedures for the field staff to follow when the contract began. As if that weren't enough, they had no one that knew how to construct a ten-city-wide area network for them to operate their business remotely and to funnel their data back to the central office. I began the process of provisioning circuits, purchasing $320,000 worth of hardware to build the infrastructure, installing the servers with their operating systems and their supporting software. All the while, I was continuing to write code for the new system they would use. Finally, the hardware started to show up, but the organization had no relationships with companies near their remote offices so that the hardware could be installed. So, I took my laptop and coded on the road as my dad drove me around the circumference of a 34,000 square-mile area to do the installations at each of the ten cities.

I continued this pace until July 1 when they officially took over the responsibilities of the contract. Then it really hit. They still had no money since the prepayment they received for the contract went to build their infrastructure. Because of this, I was abducted by necessity to support one hundred and fifty-three field users remotely and by myself. When any one of them had data or computer problems, it was my phone that rang. I was working fourteen-hour days at that point, but because there was no income, I could not get them to hire any employees for the IT department. It was still just me.

After keeping up this dizzying pace through September, they hired an employee to help keep the data straight. She was a lifesaver to me. But now I had to start training her while I continued to maintain everything else that was going on. I was still pumping out twelve- to fourteen-hour days and was working six days a week. This pace went on for almost the first year.

When I could really bear it no more, I started to hire employees and to bill my client for their hours. Over the course of the next two years, we built a wonderful IT staff that did phenomenal tasks. I worked closely with the president of the corporation on a number of contract-related issues and did so with pleasure. All the time and investment I had placed in that company made them my second home. I had dedicated my heart, mind and soul to them, and I was determined to make them look as good as possible.

In remuneration for my labors, I was paid a contract amount that was average for the industry in my geographic area, and they agreed to take no ownership in the software that I had written. The president and I made, and put into writing, an agreement stating that I would maintain control and ownership of the software, but that they would always have the right to a copy of the source code and a permanent license to its use. I felt this was fair since I had aspirations of selling it around the nation to other providers of similar services and it would be an ongoing source of income for me and my family.

I was permanently invited to the management meetings, where the president would meet with the vice presidents, and I was given the liberty to speak as though I were part of that organization. Beyond that, I was asked to serve on a number of special-interest teams regarding the finances and business operations of the organization. I had learned how the president thought and tried to calculate his desires before he asked for them. I gave the same attention to the field staff that he had. If I could stay one step ahead of them, then when they needed something, it would already be there waiting for them.

One day, during the administrative staff meeting, the president asked for a very specific set of reports. He specifically asked one vice president to generate the reports and to call as many others on the team to help as were necessary. The system I had written housed all the data for the reports, but he never called me for help. It was at that point that I realized there was a burgeoning problem. No matter how many times I offered to help, he very kindly told me that none was needed. After a few weeks, I was called privately into the president's office. I was instructed to sit down, and a copy of the report was thrown into my lap. "Did you have any part of this?!"

"No sir," I replied.

"I didn't think so. This isn't what I asked for. Can you give me what I want?"

"Yes sir," I again replied.

"Good. I need it by tomorrow at 10:00 a.m." It was currently about 11:30 a.m. That left me only about twelve hours of usable time to generate reports that had taken better than a week for the vice president to complete. I asked him if he understood what he was asking of me. With that, he softened and replied, "Yes. And if you can't do it, I'll understand. But, if it's possible, I'd like it done."

I left his office and started pulling statistics and crunching numbers, making graphs, tables and charts. By 9:30 a.m. the next morning I had the reports to him. I walked to his office and knocked on the brown wooden trim that encased his door. Inside sat the president with his daily Jonathan apple and half a bagel. I handed him the report and sat down in the chair to the right of his desk, a bit breathless, to see what his response would be.

"Thank you. This is exactly what I was expecting in the first place. If you'll excuse me, I need to get ready for our meeting in half an hour."

"Are you planning on using my report during your leadership meeting with your vice presidents," I asked.

"Yes, I am," he replied.

"You understand that by doing this, you will make it very difficult for me to work with your management team once the meeting is over?"

"I do," was his response. "But they have to understand that when I ask for something, I need what I asked for."

That 10:00 a.m. meeting was tense for me as he took copies of the reports I had created, tossed them in the center of the table, and asked each vice president to take a copy. He then said, "This is what I expected. Why should I have to ask Bryan for this report when you should have done it right in the first place?"

Why do I share all of this with you? Because I want you to understand that I had dedicated myself completely to this organization. I had sacrificed my time, my family, my life and even my professional reputation to create a large piece of who they were, to make them work and to keep them running. They had no one else, and they were convinced that by the time they found someone else, anyone coming in would take way too long to learn how they did business. I invested everything I was into this organization and was included at levels that no one else before me had enjoyed. I was trusted by the president himself and was mentored by him. I gave this organization all that I was and didn't hold back. I took ownership in their purpose and mission. There was only a handful of their almost six hundred employees who gave anything close to what I did in an effort to see them prosper. I had dedicated myself to them wholly and sacrificially.

As the next couple of years went by, the organization began to change. Person by person, those that I served with when we started this grand venture retired or left. The president was succeeded by a man whose friendship I enjoyed tremendously. I had the opportunity to work closely with this new president for almost a year until the next change happened. The chief financial officer, another one of the people I had worked with from the beginning, left the company. I had reported to him on site, and he was the staff member who ruled over the IT department. Remember, I was a contractor that they had hired to do the work. But, even though I was not on their payroll, I was given extreme latitude from this man to run things on his behalf and to prosper their interests.

Once he was gone and his replacement was hired, things began to change swiftly. I'll not go into great detail at this point, but suffice it to say that it was obvious I was on the way out. No matter how hard I tried to communicate, it availed nothing. In a day, I was excluded and shunned. When everything had reached its finality, we could never come to an agreement on what a contract for continuing services would look like, and after thirteen years of a business relationship, we decided to go our separate ways.

After all the time and labor—after all the work and sweat—I was discarded like a tattered pair of shoes. Nothing I could do would yield results. Over and over again I would try to communicate with them, but my efforts were repaid with falsehoods and misinformation. Rumors were started about me that I chose not to refute. It was horrible and amazing at the same time—that the principal leadership in an organization I had dealt with honorably for thirteen years could turn so distasteful was mind-boggling to me. I had lost all trust in the leadership and knew at that point it was finished. Where there is no trust, there can be no relationship.

> I felt betrayed, left behind, hated, unwanted and abused.

In a final effort to close the door and not burn the bridge, I apologized for anything that I might have done to offend them. When I said words that were misinterpreted, I made a point to try and properly interpret them for the listener and to apologize for those as well. On numerous occasions, I asked for the chance to learn what I had done to deserve the treatment I was being given, but no one would return my requests. E-mails and phone calls were ignored. Finally, after three months of appealing to the then-reigning president, I received what appeared to be a form letter in the mail that said, "With the changing of the leadership in any organization, there by necessity comes a change in vision and direction." That was the only explanation I received, and to this day, I know no more.

That was by far the hardest professional experience I have endured in my career. I felt betrayed, left behind, hated, unwanted and abused. To have given all that I did for as long as I did; to develop a system that, at state audit time, had an error percentage of .003 percent; to invest so heavily into their operation and mission and then to be aborted was more gut-wrenching than anything I've experienced before or since.

For me, the breakthrough came almost a year later, and I talk about that in the next chapter. But, to you who are on the precipice of change, or if you find yourself in a similar situation where you feel that your worth is being challenged or that you are being discarded and have no control over what is happening, let me encourage you with the following thoughts:

1. There's more out there than you know. When my work with this client was done and I had fulfilled my responsibilities to them, I took a month off to unwind and recuperate. During my hiatus, I decided that God was not surprised by what had happened, and I knew that I could trust Him with my future. I began resting in that truth. After a month off, on August 2, I went out and started knocking on doors to find new clients. Within two days, all the hours that I had dedicated to my previous client were consumed by a handful of other clients that needed what I had to offer. That handful of clients remains to this day. What I lost in one form I gained in a beautiful other. You don't know what wonderful thing is waiting at the end of your current experience. Hold on to it lightly.

2. Do your best not to treat others the way you are being treated. This is by far the hardest part. There were conversations that I had with the new staff of that organization that caught me off-guard. But, I watched my words as closely as I could, and despite the sting of their lips, I tried not to bite back. The very few times that my humanity prevailed, I formally apologized and asked them to forgive me. Despite what this client did or didn't offer to me in the way of apologies, I chose to forgive them for what they had done and said. I made it my severe responsibility to leave that client with no unrepented wrongs or sly words outstanding.

3. Leave graciously. If you are convinced that you are on the way out and you've tried everything you can to repair the situation to no avail, leave gracefully. It was blatantly obvious that when June 30 came, I would have no further relationship with this client. So, starting in the middle of April, I began to gradually decrease my presence, and by May first, I had silently left their facility with no argument or fanfare. When the time came for me to depart for good, I sent an e-mail to some of my co-workers, telling them that opportunities were changing and encouraging them to continue on with the good work they were doing.

4. Don't try to justify yourself to your coworkers. In my case, the only person that really knew what happened when I stopped working with that client was a vice president with whom I was close. My reputation meant and still means more to me than any amount of cash or any possession I may own. Overall, I made it a point neither to relive nor repeat the unkind words that were spoken to or about me. I also made it a point not to defame anyone at that organization. When people would ask me about specifics that they had heard, I simply asked them to judge anything they were hearing against what they knew about me as a person. It is the morose side of human nature which shows that if people choose to believe defamatory things about you, no amount of self-justification in their presence

will clear your record. When you are gone, they will continue to believe as they will. All you can do is to try your best to stay above reproach and leave the rest to time. The truth will always outlive a lie.

5. Give yourself time to heal. Once you've gotten to the end of an experience, give yourself room to work through the grief and emotion that may come at its conclusion; it's all part of the process. Your feelings may range from a simple case of "who cares?" to a bereavement as great as losing a family member to a fatal accident. However you may process the closing of a relationship, just remember to be kind to yourself as you walk through anger, denial, frustration, loss, fear, forgiveness, patience and trust. Whether your relationship is with a person or an organization, the demise of a close relationship brings pain and adjustment. If you find it unbearable, find someone to talk with about your struggle. Don't try to bear it alone. A good friend or a pastor can help you bear the emotional load.

EIGHTEEN

YOU ARE BEING PAID FOR YOUR JOB

For you, it's another day in the trenches. You have invested great energy in refining your skill and talent. You are determined to be the best at what you do, and you want to show your employer that you are a valuable asset. To do this, you choose to work hard and shut up. You invest yourself in your employer and take responsibility for the work you produce. If something isn't right, you work until it is—whether it takes all night or not. What you do is of great benefit to your employer—you know it, and they know it. Suddenly and without warning, your job changes. Overnight, you feel like you've been betrayed. Because of this, your attitude starts to sour.

You are looking at it from the vantage point of someone who gave and gave and then proved himself. You are feeling that you were owed more than just a paycheck; you were owed respect. But, in the real world, that doesn't happen. You have to constantly remind yourself of this one thing: *you are being paid for your job*. When you signed on to work for your employer, you agreed to give them the best you have in return for a paycheck. Nowhere in any of the documentation you signed did your employer state, "We will honor you at all times; we will esteem you at all times; we will worship you for your excellent work; we will never change your job; we will never let you go."

Once you realize that your struggle for perfection and importance is between you and God Himself, you will find great liberty. You no longer need to walk in fear of losing your job; you no longer need to prove yourself to your employer. You simply have to choose to be the best you can possibly be, to enjoy your job and to give it all you have. Then, if the vision, purpose or leadership of your employer changes and you are no longer needed as part of their new team, you can be at peace, knowing that you have no regrets and that your employer was enhanced by your previous work. Don't see it as a slap in the face or as a way of saying you're worthless. Instead, choose to see it as graduation day. You get to move on to the next book in your life-long curriculum of learning, and you get to bring your skill and talent to another agency. Just be certain that you do everything you can to have a good separation and try not to hold tightly to what you have. Remember, if you begin to feel bitter or betrayed, remind yourself that you made an agreement to exchange your talent for money. Tell yourself, "This is no big deal. I was paid for my work. We're even. They don't owe me a thing. Our agreement is complete and finished." Then, let it go, travel to your next stop and start giving and learning again. After all, you have drive, ambition and talent.

Let me end this section with a small personal illustration. By now, you've read about a long-term client who, due to internal changes, became a poor fit for me. When I no longer had them as a client, I went through a time of depression. It was intoxicating working for them, and they were one of the most enjoyable organizations I have ever worked for. I put 1800 hours a year into their company. When I no longer had them, I started looking to replace that 1800 hours of work. I took a month off to recuperate, took my family to the forest and donated a couple of weeks to a youth camp, giving instead of thinking about myself. When I came back, I began the process of recruiting new clients. On August 2, I started letting people know that I had openings, and on August 3 at 2:00 p.m., I was completely booked again. All of those 1800 hours were filled, and I continued on as though nothing had ever happened. Just know that the God of the universe has you in His sights and He will not forget you. It's okay to believe. Just be willing to trust, to let go of the past, to remember that there's no debt left outstanding, to throw your shoulders back, to stand tall, to take your newly earned diploma from the hands (or teeth) of your current employer and to head off to what lies ahead.

NINETEEN

ALWAYS PROTECT YOUR NAME AND YOUR WORD

"Son, always honor your word and protect your family name!" My father drilled this into me from my earliest memories, and I am doing the same thing with my children. This is a primal value that has been lost over the past forty years, and which, I believe, needs to be reconstructed in our world if we are to ever get past the quick sands of carelessness and selfishness.

When you do your job, when you say you will do something, when you approach other people, when you carry your conversations, do you concern yourself with how it will affect not only what people think of you, but what they think of your parents, your siblings, your spouse and your children? What if I told you of a woman who was famous for bringing compassion and love to millions of orphaned children? What if I told you that she spent every penny of her life's savings to bring food and clothing to these children, whose families were horribly murdered? What if I told you that she herself lost her life in the course of feeding thousands of three- and four-year-old children who could not fend for themselves? How would you feel about her? Then, how would you feel if I told you that her son was a serial killer responsible for the strangulation and murder of thirty-one women across the country? Would you still feel the same? Or would the fact that her son was such a wretch depreciate all the amazing things that she performed in her life?

How do you feel when you hear the last name Bundy? How do you feel when you hear the last name Manson? How do you feel when you hear the name Oswald? What about the name Stallone? What about the name Van Damme? I've given you names that may cause you to remember specific people in history. Your recollections bring back feelings of anger, fear, frustration, excitement, joy and triumph, and yet, you don't even have a first name associated with any of them.

Your family name incites the same types of feelings with people you are around—people who you work with and people who you play with. What feelings are they experiencing when they hear your name? Are they feelings of joy, of knowing your faithfulness, of knowing your goodness, of feeling secure just knowing that you are around? Or are they feelings of disdain, feelings of frustration, feelings of bitterness and anger? Just remember that the groundwork you lay for the perception of your name will go well into the future, and it will affect everyone in your current generation with the same name, whether they did anything to deserve the treatment or not.

As a small example, let me share that I have an older sister. She carried a wonderful reputation all the way through school. By the time I reached middle and senior high school, I didn't have to work very hard to get approval with the teachers and staff. They all assumed that since sis was who she was, and since I was her brother, then I must be okay. The same was true with my dad. For his whole life, he has done almost all his business on a handshake, and his word is as good as gold. Because of that, many doors have opened for me that I never had to push on, all because of my dad's good name. I reaped the rewards of their care and concern and of their diligence in protecting our family name. How well are you doing? It's never too late to start. Make your family proud, and prepare the way for the generations that will follow you, even if it requires financial or other types of loss for you. Always protect your family name and watch over your word—they are two of the two most valuable intangibles you have.

TWENTY

WE ALL NEED MENTORS

There are so many things we don't know. That seems to be the nature of life. We try and try. We gain knowledge and understanding, and yet, when we look around, there is someone more adept, better mannered, more professional, more gifted and more successful than we are or perhaps may ever be. To reach beyond ourselves, it becomes necessary to grab someone's hand and ask him to pull us up out of the sludge that we may have sunk into. That someone is a mentor.

If you've never enjoyed the company of a mentor, you are missing a great joy in life. A mentor is someone who has already been there or who knows, by experience or training, why you shouldn't go in the first place. A mentor is someone who you can trust and who will be truthful with you about your actions and plans. It is someone who can pull wisdom from the vast resources of his experience, knowledge and observations and apply it to what you are learning or to what you may need in an effort to lift you up. I have been honored to have a few mentors in my life who have contributed to the man that I have become.

If you want to be more than you are, find someone who is what you want to be. See if you can take him to lunch, and then let him teach you who he is and how he got where he is now. It's not very often that people refuse to share their life experiences with you, especially if they are successful. If you have the freedom, be bold and ask these people to mentor you. The least that can happen is that they decline. If they agree, you have just begun a new learning career in your life, and you have taken the next step toward becoming what you aspire to be.

TWENTY-ONE

WORKING WITH A CONTROLMONGER

One of the most difficult things I ever had to do was to work with a person who was a controlmonger. Let me start by saying that the controlmonger is not a wicked person worthy of dungeon imprisonment: they have a tremendous amount of value to bring to an organization. In the world of cheese, you find a cheesemonger to help you choose the perfect cheese to tantalize your taste buds. In the world of fish, you find a fishmonger to identify the perfect texture and flavor for your gourmet dish. In the world of control, you will find a controlmonger knows virtually everything there is about control in the world that is most familiar to him. I am a recovering controlmonger and will probably be one for the rest of my life. The only reason that I am now able to let go and delegate is because I came to the realization that I had an abuse problem and have worked through some self-prescribed treatment. So, as I continue writing about the specifics of my experience with a good friend of mine, who is a controlmonger, I place myself among her number.

My friend is very possessive about her work—so possessive that she frightens people away from her. Out of the office, you'd never know that she was obsessive with her job because she is very relaxed. At work, though, she becomes a driven, controlling perfectionist who must have her finger on all things at all times. If a decision is made without her knowledge, she will assemble the firing squad.

When I first began to work with her, I was scared. She would rant and rave and throw a fit over something that was in error. Others in the office had resorted to waiting until she went to lunch or to the restroom so that they could run in and put a sticky note on her desk to avoid speaking with her in person. Finally, one day it sank in for me. The controlmonger is controlling because she is insecure about what is happening around her and because she doesn't want her name associated with something that could fail. The controlmonger will labor and stress over everything in an attempt to keep her name safe and to be certain that her security level is as high as possible. Her goal? To make criticism an impossibility. When I realized this truth, it changed forever how I would deal with controlling people. From that point to now, I began using the same response in an uncomfortable situation with a controlling person. I wait for him to take a breath, and I say, "Hey. I'm on your side. I'm for you, not against you. I'm here to make things better for you. Just tell me what you want and I'll do everything I can to make it happen. Just name it."

Amazingly, I have found that offering firm support and encouragement goes a long way in the eyes of a controlmonger. In the case of my friend, when I would do this, her demeanor would change and she would begin to smile again. This happened because she was being told that I was on her side and that she got to use my resources to get her job done. When you do this, the controlmonger feels better because you have expressed interest by investing in her life and her job. By helping her achieve her main goal—namely, a sense of security and the value of excellence attached to her name. Just remember, though, doing it once isn't enough. The controlmonger needs ongoing trust and encouragement. The chances are extremely high that you will have to do this over and over again. Don't give up, though. Even though a controlmonger can be difficult to work with, he is also one of the best people to have on your side when you are looking for allies because he is usually perceived as very dedicated and observant.

TWENTY-TWO

A MAN UNDER AUTHORITY

So often we taint real authority by coloring it with our memories of abused authority. When you hear the word authority, it shouldn't conjure up feelings of betrayal, frustration and bitterness. Instead, it should engender a sense of safety and security. If it doesn't, you may have to adjust your opinion of what authority really is.

Authority isn't a gauge of a person's perfection or her ability to understand any level of the business she works in. It has no reference to intelligence level or skill. Authority is the endowed ability to make decisions and to take consequences, whether they are good or bad. Authority means that for whatever reason, someone in a higher level of control decided that someone in a lower level of control needed to be empowered with certain rights and that he or she is being trusted to act on behalf of that higher level until told otherwise. And while authority can cause problems when it's abused, you should learn to rest in it and allow the person working in the position of authority the right to make decisions and experience consequences without having to prove herself to you.

In my dealings with different organizations, I have been privy to the complaints and observations of a number of staff at all different levels. One such client employed a man who was operating as a vice president. He was lambasted for his control issues and for being a "yes" man. But my observation was quite different. Did he fall prey to corporate politics? Certainly, he did at times. But the reason he was a "yes" man was because this was the type of authority the president of that corporation needed while he was away on travels. Because the president managed by personal and specific controls, he didn't need someone who would second-guess his decision-making process. That president needed someone to be his eyes and ears while he was gone, who could assess the situation for him, report on it, get directions from him and then carry them out, irrespective of the approval rating by others in the organization. In my estimation of things, he was performing exactly the way he was supposed to. He did what he was told and experienced the results of his obedience. He could have bucked the system when he disagreed with the president, but he chose to remain loyal and to allow the president to decide and to create the corporate experience. He shared his concerns with the president when it was appropriate, but if he disagreed, he never did it in the public square; it was always behind closed doors. And when the door was opened and they walked out, it was impossible to tell that they were ever at odds with each other.

Authority can be a freeing thing, whether it's under someone who is abusive with it or free with it. Here is the key. Walk into your work environment and only make decisions in the sphere in which you have been given control. If it's out of your control, don't go there; don't even offer your comments unless asked by the authority over that sphere of influence. If you aren't asked for input, don't offer it. When the time is right for you to shine, it will happen naturally. Just make it your focus to be the best you can possibly be at whatever you set your mind to. If you run into something that is beyond you, don't be afraid to defer to the authority above you and ask him to make the decision or to walk through the decision-making process with you. That is what he is there for. Above all, don't disagree with your authority in the public arena. If you disagree with a decision that has been made, and you've been granted the ability to approach your authority and to speak freely of such matters, be open and share your concerns behind closed doors. If you have not been granted this freedom, your only response should be, "What would you like me to do? I'm here for you." Do a good job of fulfilling this law, and when you are in a position of authority, you'll get to enjoy the fruits of others doing it for you.

TWENTY-THREE

THE EYES HAVE IT

The month was October. I was following I-90 eastward from Seattle, Washington. The final destination was a small town nestled in the heart of the central plains. As I drove through the upper portion of Idaho and Montana, I was amazed at the absolute beauty of the landscape. The foliage sported the most surreal fall colors. Clouds of scarlet and orange topped the mountainous horizon. The colors were so brilliant that they seemed to have been mixed by hand. Wisps of white trailed downward as the clouds appeared to unravel and fall to the ground. A breeze was blowing gently from the south, and the only sound to be heard was the violin-like chirp of crickets, an occasional bass note from a toad and a gentle chorus whistled by a few birds. As I sat on the hood of my car, absolutely overwhelmed by what I was seeing, I could not imagine how anything could be more beautiful.

A few years later, I found myself in a twenty-four-by-fourteen-foot room with my wife lying on a hospital bed. All of our planning and preparation had brought us to this day. As the doctor looked at my newborn child, he happily told me, "It's a boy." Immediately, my wife and I began to laugh and cry at the same time. As I looked down at that little baby, my heart was overwhelmed with the most inexpressible sense of joy, love, excitement and fear. This happened again two years later as we saw the beauty and near perfection of our little girl as she was born. Staring down into the faces of these amazing gifts, I could not imagine how anything could be more beautiful.

If you had been with me in Idaho and Montana, would you have seen the beauty I described, or would you have seen just another pile of rocks on a partly cloudy day? If you had been in the room at the hospital, would you have seen the amazement of a child's birth, or would it have been yet one more crying kid? How do you see what is around you? Depending on how you answer this question, you may have found the binding thread to everything written in this book.

We are each responsible for setting our own focus. We each choose where our own vision lies. We each determine if we will look deeply into the eyes of our tomorrow or only at the surface of our calendars; at the asphalt of the highway as it stretches out beyond our sight, or down at the pavement just under our feet. It is how we see and where we look that determines how we act. If we invest our focus and attention solely on the immediate, we will only experience immediate gratification, and we will be saddened by our future when we get there. I am someone who believes that the life we construct on this earth can only be valuable when we invest in the lives of others and when we develop an accountability to the eternal. Without exception, the basis for every sound decision we make must come from the act of investing our love and our lives in those around us and from developing a grounded accountability to immovable truth.

Where are you in the process of determining your focus? Have you ever looked past your life and into the expanse of eternity to make your decisions? If you are not in the habit of doing so, let me help you refine your field of view. Think about the amazing sunset and the cloud-covered sky I described earlier and then start with this primary question: The clouds are made of billions of atoms—where did the very first atom of gas come from? Has it always been? Or, was it somehow made from nothing? No conversation about anything real can be supported without first answering this primary question. Ignoring it will not make it go away and only issues a warrant for ignorance.

Every one of us must start at this primary question and build our beliefs and disbeliefs, our sight and our blindness, from there.

Once you have sought until you can seek no more and have found the answer to this question, go to question number two: What about those things which we cannot see but which affect our daily lives, like the physical laws of gravity, lift and magnetism, and our civil laws, which determine right and wrong? Why is it wrong to steal? Why is it wrong to lie? What makes it wrong to take another person's life from them whenever we want? Why are these things punishable instead of applauded or encouraged? How could such orderly, invisible and powerful laws come from nowhere and proceed from nothing? Have they always existed as real, yet invisible, or do they, too, have an origin? Was there ever a time in the past when nothing existed, be it visible or invisible? If so, where did existence begin? You see, I believe these questions establish the basis for eternity—that there was a place of existence before the first atom of gas appeared and that there will be a place of existence after the last atom of gas expires. Please, don't skim over this or shrug it off. Don't consider this thought process as "too deep." I would suggest that it is more uncomfortable than deep.

Without shame, I admit that I believe just as our nation's forefathers did: that we have a creator, and that through the perfection of His mind's eye, He has made what we see from what was not visible. We see His personality and character in all that is naturally created and the reflection of His face in a man named Jesus.

Every chapter you have read finds its value in the absolute person of Jesus as the Son of the God. He created everything we know to be real. Every thing we see is held together by Him, and without His intervention, it would all fall apart. Every rule of order and propriety and every rule of good and honorable relationship is a characteristic of God Almighty and was exhibited to us through the sending of His son, Jesus.

With this as my foundation, when I use my eyes to look ahead into the future, I see a day that has been given to every man. I see a point in eternity where we will have the honor or the horror of standing before the God of the universe to account for the life we have invested on this earth. I see a day of great elation for some and a day of great grief for others. My fervent vision of this day drives me to love people in all circumstances and to willingly concede my life to the rule of His son, Jesus. I am convinced that there is no other way to find forgiveness in God's eyes for the innumerable travesties that I have contemplated and completed other than to willingly throw myself on His mercy and to trust wholly in Jesus as my attorney-at-law upon my trial date. As I look ahead, I know that it will be His intervention alone that will save me from whatever unspeakable outcome would have otherwise overtaken me.

My eyes are set on the eternal and on what is expected of me as I journey in that direction. My vision is on the absolute character of God as my template for relationship and life. My foundation is unshakable because it is based on the example of the Son of God Himself, who came not only to show me the way to His father, but also to lead by His example. As I set my eyes on Him, I gladly follow and pursue what He has determined is important: that we should love our coworkers, that we should not gossip, that we should honor our word and watch over it to make it happen. He has determined that we should respect the lives of others, giving them dignity and offering them respect, no matter the lifestyle they lead; that we should give our finances and our time—even if it hurts; that we should forgive others—even if they don't ask for it. He has decided that we should set boundaries in our lives so that the beautiful and important parts are not overlooked; that we should respect our family name and invest in it so that future generations will have a legacy; that we should be teachable and ready to listen; that we would seek the truth and never quit seeking until we can go no further; that we should take a position of humility—esteeming others above ourselves and looking for their betterment above our own. Is this how you would like to be treated? Will you discount these things purely because I've related them back to the person and character of Jesus? Or will you consider setting your eyes upon them as the truth and examining the uncomfortable?

Where, then, are your eyes? What is your driving force? I've elaborated mine; I have set my eyes upon what I expect to win for a prize, and then I have set my pace and begun to run toward it. What do you have in sight? What is your prize? Is it worth what you are putting into it? Is it so valuable that you would give your life for it? I hope so, because you *are* giving your life for it.

Let me close with these final words. Each of us invests his life with some end in sight, be it an inch or a mile down the road. That which is most important to us receives our time, our money and our emotion. None of us is alone in this. We all have limited resources that we are responsible for managing. How are you gauging your success? Is it by things that will disappear on your deathbed or by things that will succeed your passing? Are you looking only at the current hour and the few that follow, or are you looking up repetitively at the horizon of eternity to see if you are still on the road? Are you successfully handling your relationships, or are you leaving a trail of hateful and hurting people in your wake? Have you created a system to see if you are making progress, or are you simply hoping that you will arrive? Is the prize you are striving for immovable, or can it be stolen, destroyed or taken out of your reach? As you answer these questions and reflect upon the value of all that you have read, I hope you are challenged to dig deeper into your soul, to stretch farther into your future and to try harder as you deepen and perfect your relationships. As you pursue change in your own life and evaluate all that you hold dear, I hope you are always grounded in immutable truth that will guide you, and that you produce a legacy that will live on for generations. And, when you finally arrive at that place called "the future," bringing with you all the people and the lessons you've learned along the way, may you look around and be able to say, "I can't imagine how anything could be more beautiful."